John Fuller was born in 1937, [...]
Oxford. He is married, with [...]
runs the Sycamore Press. H[...]
poems, *Fairground Music* (196[...], [...]
Cannibals and Missionaries (1972). He has written a number of plays
and songs for children in collaboration with the composer Bryan
Kelly, edits *Nemo's Almanac*, and has published criticism, including
A Reader's Guide to W. H. Auden and *The Sonnet*. He lives for part
of the year in North Wales.

Peter Levi was born in 1931, and met Adrian Mitchell and John
Fuller at Oxford in the fifties. He is a member of the Jesuit order,
a Roman Catholic priest, and a former member of the British
School of Archaeology at Athens. He is tutor in classical languages
and literature at Campion Hall, Oxford. His publications include
The Gravel Ponds (1961), *Fresh Water, Sea Water* (1966) and *The
Light-Garden of the Angel King* (1972). He has translated (with R.
Milner-Gulland) Yevtushenko for the Penguin Modern European
Poets, and *Pausanias: Guide to Greece* for the Penguin Classics.

Adrian Mitchell was born in 1932 and has published several novels
and books of poems. They include *Fantasy Poets No. 24* (1955),
Poems (1964), *Out Loud* (1968), *Ride the Nightmare* (1971), *If You
see Me Comin'* (1962) and *The Bodyguard* (1970). Mr Mitchell has
also written some plays including *Tyger* (an L.P. record has been
issued of its songs) and *Tamburlane the Mad Hen*; and he has adapted
in verse Peter Weiss's *Marat/Sade*.

Penguin Modern Poets

22

JOHN FULLER

PETER LEVI

ADRIAN MITCHELL

Penguin Books

Penguin Books Ltd, Harmondsworth, Middlesex, England
Penguin Books Australia Ltd, Ringwood, Victoria, Australia

—

This selection first published 1973
Copyright © Penguin Books Ltd, 1973

—

Made and printed in Great Britain by
C. Nicholls & Company Ltd
Set in Monotype Garamond

Contents

CONTENTS

CONTENTS

ADRIAN MITCHELL

CONTENTS

Acknowledgements

The poems by John Fuller are taken from *Fairground Music*, 1961, and *The Tree that Walked*, 1967, both published by Chatto & Windus, and *Cannibals and Missionaries*, 1972, Secker & Warburg.

The poems by Peter Levi are taken from *The Gravel Ponds*, 1960, *Water Rock and Sand*, 1962, and *Fresh Water, Sea Water*, 1966, all published by Raven Press (André Deutsch), and *Pancakes for the Queen of Babylon*, 1968, *Life is a Platform*, 1971, and *Death is a Pulpit*, 1971, all published by Anvil Press.

The poems by Adrian Mitchell are taken from *Poems*, 1964, Jonathan Cape, *Out Loud*, 1968, Cape Goliard, and *Ride the Nightmare*, 1971, Jonathan Cape.

JOHN FULLER

from Fairground Music (1961)

Fairy Tale

Blushing, she fled: no one was on her side.
She could not bear the whistle and the slap,
The fustian prospect of a farmer's lap.
Her father moped. Her sisters swore. She cried,
Dreamed of the Prince, neglected all her tasks,
And now had run away, but not for long:
The wood was frightful as a wig, as wrong
As her own hearth. Soon she returned, through masks
Of mist. Her heart jumped at the stir that took
Her eye: the royal hounds sagged in the porch,
Their tongues like shoehorns. Someone waved a torch.
Hardly believing, breathless, she ran to look –
But worse than all the sniggers of the wood,
The waiting Prince was ugly, pale and good.

A Kiss in Galloway

Sea, buttoned snails and catapulted gulls,
Small world turned over and over on itself:
China and crystal on the cottage shelf,
The fire-reflecting brass and stranded hulls
In pale landscapes, steaming articles
For walking in the waves draped round the hearth
Like priestly robes. Coming back up the path
With beer, you make that gesture which annuls
Once more what gracelessness our history has,
And in the twilight where the butterfly
Unfolds her carpet beauty, slowly, as slow
As too-rich dew creeps on dead summer's grasses,
We seal our fatal promise to defy
That we may be delivered into woe.

The Statue

Your buttonholes for eyes, your solemn face,
The golden hair against your sleeping back:
This is no other time, no other place,
A moment certain as the almanac,
Vivid as weather, quiet as the deep,
As innocent as hands that curl in sleep.

For dreams disguise our wish to be awake
With bells, lagoons and squalls of tinsel trees.
In dreams you are not cruel, yet can't fake
An understanding of your cruelties.
Later, we're on the road: our object is
To judge a dead art's possibilities.

The radiator choked with butterflies,
We reach the city in a thumbed-down car
And I discover that the staring eyes
And cool lips of the promised statue are,
Though fabulous, immortalized in stone,
Less rare and calm and perfect than your own.

For, in the camera's illusion, he
Preserved a moment from a laughing past,
A consolation for inconstancy,
Carefree, amorous, dynamic, vast,
Making a message on a mantelpiece,
A famous face sent by a friend from Greece.

But when we view the postcard subject fresh,
Gazing from curls to reconstructed toes,

Gone is the gentle and the human flesh,
Slyly dramatic in a talking pose:
Instead I see, and think I understand
The broken smile, whips in the missing hand.

Morvin

Serpents exploded, open balconies
Offered their gazers to the bursting stars
And sparks like worlds fell slowly down
Upon the statues and the waiting cars.

My limbs moved tightly underneath the lights
And I remembered awe, excitement, shots.
Lanterns were ikons, rockets streaming blood,
The royal crest upon the chamber pots.

My nerves were better the next day, but as
I strolled in rain along the promenade,
I caught my breath again, chancing to glimpse
A tram-race in the wet, a red haired guard.

'Morvin!' I murmured, and the smell of fruit
Rose warmly to my nostrils, but I knew
That this was but a token of my state
Of feebleness, making imagined true.

Before the blood I had a solemn role
In the land: a statesman useful to the King
For striding on the great stairhead to cry
'Back with the greasy mob!' or keep a ring

For squeezing at the bottom of a writ
To get a burgher killed. In better days,
(Ah, it was fresh in the North!) I walked disguised
In silent streets, guilty, but proud always

To glimpse the workings of my 'famous' laws.
(Out of his kitchen peeped the smirking cook
To see the clients satisfied. Behind,
Insidiously, where he did not look,

Flames crept.) The Crown was gutted in its bed.
More blood was got ... Now I am stripped of robes
And strangely, too, of self: I scratch and wheeze;
Fingers which lopped, now sadly tug at, lobes;

And in this warmer land to which I flew,
Lucky to live, I sip aperitifs,
Chat with the guests, write in my attic room
Inventions for my loss of place, my grief.

Now it is dark again. I feel some stir
Within me. Is it over? Am I dead
Indeed? Perhaps I should have been that stabber,
Been that revolution's brilliant head,

Whom I see in whiteness, whom I hold
As gangling, filthy, vital, like a wink
Regrettably ignored, haunting: Morvin!
(Whom perhaps I only think I think),

O Morvin! As the silent puffs of cannon
Move like thistleseed across the hill,
I sit and ponder at the end of day
Upon your complex smiling presence still.

If, after one illuminating phrase,
I smash a pane, admitting the night air,
Shall I arise to stormy deeds of nothing
Or in a mirror see *your* glowing hair?

You thrill with your suggestions like a child:
Prompting my arm, you ruin the gathered page.
You are the startling conscience of us all,
The poking finger to a nervous age.

Edwardian Christmas

Father's opinion of savages
And dogs, a gay Bloomsbury epigram:
'The brutes may possibly have souls,' he says,
'But reason, no. Nevertheless, I am
Prepared not to extend this to my spouse
And children.' This demands a careful pity:
Poor Father! Whooping and romping in their house,
A holiday from ruin in the City.
His wit falls flat, his tie just will not tie.
The dog's in chains, the reasonable books
Grazed by his children as they learn to fly.
He takes his dear wife's arm (his hands grow hooks).
Pirates and pudding! Come, such cruelty!

His beard is branching like a burning tree.

Essay on Spenser

Clownish without his armour, he
Clamped down his umbriere. His sword
Knocking against the trees, men fell
About him, headless, twitching. His
Thick heart jumping, he plunged through
The steaming wood until against
His Lady's Tower, sword down, he gasped
The rune to move the man-high stone
That blocked her keeping, up again
He raced the spiral shaft and beat
In rage the spellbound oak. And died.
For a splintered mirror spoilt her plan
To save him from the littered plain,
And all that night fell frogs and rain.

In a Railway Compartment

Oxford to London, 1884:
Against the crimson arm-rest leaned a girl
Of ten, holding a muff, twisting a curl,
Drumming her heels in boredom on the floor
Until a white-haired gentleman who saw
She hated travelling produced a case
Of puzzles: 'Seven Germans run a race . . .
Unwind this maze, escape the lion's paw . . .
The princess must be lowered by her hair . . .'
The train entered a tunnel, shrieking, all
The lights went out and when he took her hand
She was the princess in the tower and
A lion faced her on the moonlit wall
Who roared and reached and caught and held her there.

Song

You don't listen to what I say.
When I lean towards you in the car
You simply smile and turn away.

It's been like this most of the day,
Sitting, and sipping, bar after bar:
You don't listen to what I say.

You squeeze a lemon from a tray,
And if you guess how dear you are
You simply smile and turn away.

Beyond the hairline of the bay
The steamers call that shore is far.
You don't listen to what I say:

Surely there's another way?
The waiter brings a small guitar.
You simply smile and turn away.

Sometimes I think you are too gay,
Smiling and smiling, hour after hour.
You don't listen to what I say.
You simply smile and turn away.

Alex at the Barber's

He is having his hair cut. Towels are tucked
About his chin, his mop scalped jokingly.
The face in the mirror is his own face.

The barber moves and chats among the green
And methylated violet, snipper-snips,
Puts scissors down, plugs in a plaited flex,

And like a surgeon with his perfumed hands
Presses the waiting skull and shapes the base.
He likes having his hair cut, and the man

Likes cutting it. The radio drones on.
The eyes in the mirror are his own eyes.
While the next chair receives the Demon Blade,

A dog-leg razor nicks a sideburn here;
As from a sofa there a sheet is whisked
And silver pocketed. The doorbell pings.

The barber, frowning, grips the ragged fringe
And slowly cuts. Upon the speckled sheet
The bits fall down and now his hair is cut.

The neighing trams outside splash through the rain.
The barber tests the spray for heat and rubs
Lemon shampoo into his spiky hair.

Bent with his head above the running bowl,
Eyes squeezed shut, he does not see the water
Gurgle and sway like twisted sweetpaper

Above the waste, but, for a moment, tows
A sleigh of polished silver parrots through
Acres of snow, exclaiming soundlessly.

Then towel round head. Head swung gently up.
Eyes padded. As the barber briskly rubs,
The smile in the mirror is his own smile.

Girl with Coffee Tray

Slipping, she fell into the sitting-room,
For one gay second noticed what was there:
The salmon cushion on the lashed cane chair;
The frail greenness of apples in a gloom
Of chalk wall; round her head the watery boom
Of stool logs, crags and waves of hessian sea
Where driftwood pencils and books floated. She
Considered vaguely that the arching plume
Of her white cat's tail, too, was oceanic.
The sofa creaked. Cups smashed to smithereens.
The cat mewed like a gull, bounced off in panic.
Her feet still sprawling on the hall's wax tiles,
She cried. The seabed carpet stretched for miles
Where she lay drowning in the blues and greens.

from The Tree That Walked (1967)

The Cook's Lesson

When the King at last could not manage an erection,
The tables were wiped down and a banquet prepared.
The Cook was a renegade, a master of innuendo,
And was later hanged for some imaginary subversion,
Found laughing in the quarter of the filthy poor.
This, had we known it, was to be his last banquet,
And as such was fittingly dissident and experimental.
Often he had confided to us the tenets of his craft,
How a true artist is obsessed with the nature of his material,
And must make evident the process of creation in
    preference
To the predictable appearance of the finished product.
The charcoal-burners were lit, the porcelain laid
And the simple broths prepared in which the meal was
    enacted,
For this was a living meal, a biological history of food.
I cannot remember much. We sweated and fainted and
    were revived
With fragrant towels. We ate furiously and were
    rewarded
With knowledge of a kind we did not even recognize.
Spawn in the luke gruel divided, gilled and finned,
Swam down flowered channels to the brink of oil
And fell to the plate. Before our eyes
The litter spurted into the fire, picked out by tongs,
Eggs hatched into the soup, embryos bled,
Seeds sprouted in the spoon. As I said, we ate fast,
Far back into life, eating fast into life.

Now I understand that food is never really dead:
Frilled and forked, towered, dusted, sliced,
In mimic aspic or dispersed in sauces,
Food is something that will not willingly lie down.
The bland liquids slid over our tongues as
Heartbeats under crusts, mouthfuls of feathers.

An Exchange between the Fingers
and the Toes

Fingers:

Cramped, you are hardly anything but fidgets.
We, active, differentiate the digits:
Whilst you are merely *little toe* and *big*
(Or, in the nursery, some futile pig)
Through vital use as pincers there has come
Distinction of the *finger* and the *thumb*;
Lacking a knuckle you have sadly missed
Our meaningful translation to a *fist*;
And only by the curling of that joint
Could the firm *index* come to have a point.
You cannot punch or demonstrate or hold
And therefore cannot write or pluck or mould:
Indeed, it seems deficiency in art
Alone would prove you the inferior part.

Toes:

Not so, my friends. Our clumsy innocence
And your deft sin is the main difference
Between the body's near extremities.
Please do not think that we intend to please:
Shut in the dark, we once were free like you.
Though you enslaved us, are you not slaves, too?
Our early balance caused your later guilt,
Erect, of finding out how we were built.
Your murders and discoveries compile
A history of the crime of being agile,
And we it is who save you when you fight
Against the odds: you cannot take to flight.
Despite your fabrications and your cunning,
The deepest instinct is expressed in running.

Goodbye to the Garden

Pad-pad in the dark, the lawn's in tears
Where we somnambulate, fearful of worms,
In Andy Pandy nightclothes, needing love.

Before our hands we had what now we hedge,
And it confronts us like a crime: long after,
Seeming dull, it makes us desperate.

It must house much disaster. Something beats
Inside. It is a roof for multitudes.
Water is a fallen window in it.

And now the punctual stars converge upon it,
And the Creamola moon is seen to drown
Inside it. Well, it is time for the television

Brooding in the still room like ectoplasm.
Our present knowledge is our long disease,
Or something. Goodbye, garden. The night admires us.

Hedge Tutor

Consulting the calendar of hedges
Banked up higher than your head,
We seem to share the surprise of walking
On a riverbed.

Our hands touch the flowers, shocked:
A clutch of folded fern, a brief
Violet, crumpled like a girl's
Handkerchief.

And we lean to ourselves, and to
These rituals that love condemns
Us to, gathering until the hand
Is hot with stems.

Somewhere a long way back it began.
It spun and clustered, divided and broke.
The woods made way, your eyes softened
And the hedges spoke:

'We do not suffer. Roots are lodged.
We prophesy the past and free
The future from its curious bond
As history.

This is what we are and were.
You, like us, powerless to change,
Walk in the given garden. The rest
Time will arrange.'

Thick light and wet, a gradient's pull
Past the invisible coughing cows,

Shoes plastered with grass,
Back to the house:

Shall we be ashamed? You are scared
By the gassed turnip heads beneath a stile,
Take my arm tighter, hurry through the rain
With a homeward smile

To the timed clock and the caged flower,
The raincoats hung, the table laid,
The different books half-lit beneath
A single shade.

No one believes more than a tiny tract.
In the delirium of silence the vast extenses
Wheel inwards to you, the presumable
Spiral's axis.

Objet Trouvé: Piazza San Marco

We've seen St Mark's personal foot
Encased within a silver boot:
A window gave on to the bone
Just like an operation
Performed with grace for jewelled feet,
And though it did not seem complete
(The boot abrupt, the relic brittle)
The object made the most of little
And challenged our aesthetic sense
With a luxurious reticence.
So we imagined that it told
With gruesome tact how in the old
Days God removed his Saints with haste
From the slow martyrdoms they faced,
How Mark rose upwards through the air
Out of his feet left standing there,
How round his pretty feet they built this square.

Primary Source

The Duchess complains her children die too young,
A pastoral counterpoint to infant labour.
The Tutor sympathizes, holds his tongue,
Himself an offspring of the factory neighbour.
Blood wrestles with blood, and class with class.
Those threads of black against the hill's green throat
Which prompted her conceit, like a forged note
Damage his useful innocence. They pass
The mortgaged oaks of the old Duke's estate.
'Youth is ambitious,' she exclaims, 'age vile,
Dependent. Do not confuse my amorous fate
With history!' The Duchess turns to smile
And rests her chin, half-stern, upon his shoulder,
As if to stop him growing any older.

Landscapes of Western New York

1. Lake Chautauqua

Behind the sheeted lake the deer
Pose, whose forests pencilled-in
Contain quiet ambuscades of snow,
The tracks and berries they defend.

Skiers drop above the town
Where bubble elevators rise
And demerara tyre-treads squeeze
Their perfect diamonds, parked for lunch.

The hotel clinks its empty beer
And clocks eject the curls and slacks
To buckle juddering steel and crouch
At speed by telescoping barns.

Night sees the hotel desolated.
Smoking at a corner table
The waiters eat what no one ordered:
Soft cheese, expensive quarto steaks.

While from sedans a mile away
The skiers serenade the deer,
And in the dark the hard white lake
Stands still among delighted trees.

2. Niagara Falls

Fierce aquatic carelessness!
Your great arenas celebrate

The sensible decision of river
To undergo a sudden fate.

What struggle there has been is done.
The rapids gather for the ledge.
From ragged foam and rocks we see
How huge the force, how bulked the edge,

How ropes of crystal braided over
Quiver, continuously thick,
Spilling to thinness in the depth,
A change as skilful as a trick.

The conjuring light falls through the spray
And ghosts of equilibrists quail.
The graded colours curve down where
Imaginary barrels sail.

We look and gasp, and are deceived.
This stagey routine fails at length
To signify what it had meant:
The waters' wilful, sickening strength.

3. *Buffalo*

The metered tarmac elevates
Its clean technologies, distils
The whiff of chemicals, a mile
Of steel. And Erie shrugs the stains.

Far from the shore a city collapses
Into its suburbs: four-garage
Colonial, and shops for tartan.
Executives flop into pools.

Industry and avenue:
The civic idea pacifies
The furies. Winking boulevards
Offer a dangerous escape.

For tourists, curios and wreckers
Assert a kind of grammar, cars
Smooth past hotels coloured as cake,
A wilderness of lowered shades.

Warmed by the sobbing of the lights
We reach the core, a cut-price noon,
The taste of our solicitude,
The negro store, the golden dome.

4. *Letchworth Park*

Car horns on the scenic whorls
Puncture the coloured woods. Behind,
A weeping smoke of water spills
Through photographic crevices.

A vegetable empire drifts
Against pathetic monuments
To local rape and torturing.
The air is warm and fine with rain.

Like someone else's shoes the strange
Utensils of the pioneers:
The women come in Steinberg hats
To view the maps and dusty churns

And creep with ten-cent postcards on
The car park's sodden botany

While unfamiliar feral sounds
Disturb the undergrowth beyond.

The land is governed. The rain falls.
This love of history preserves
The sewn eyes of the Indian,
Fearless in their bright false glass!

Pictures from a '48 De Soto

1

Humped in this swart sedan, paper half-lowered,
The automatic at my side snug as a cancer,
I watch the house. Or in the house myself

Look at my wrist, insane with jealousy:
Her furs and veils lie on the front seat,
The tongue inside its curious second home.

Even banked high in snow, the engine dead,
The woven greenish braids and tassels swing.
A razored head lurches, lolls back, headlights

Shattered in the pursued and silent mirror.
The windows are shut: palms thud wildly on
The glass. Black opening mouth, the sound switched off.

2

The last owner lugged gravel, the wings
Rusted and bolted back. We drive it
Three thousand miles to the Pacific

Where the blind nude hulk, down to its canvas,
Like a slow fist hisses into the dump.
Now the yellow plates illegally decorate

The bathroom, and these, too, fetch improbable ghosts:
After days on the anvil, tanking through the dust,
We arrive at the coloured river. Our eyes hurt.

Dwarfs wrestle behind glass. Dresses
Are cut to the buttocks' cleft. Half-shaved men
Are running sheeted through the empty square.

The Pit

From the beginning, the egg cradled in pebbles,
The drive thick with fledglings, to the known last
Riot of the senses, is only a short pass.
Earth to be forked over is more patient,
Bird hungers more, flower dies sooner.

But if not grasped grows quickly, silently.
We are restless, not remembering much.
The pain is slow, original as laughter,
Reaching for all of it, hardly aware,
Beginning again and feeling for its terrain.

We were often told and still we would not listen,
And closing fingers, those accomplices,
Took comfort from a lie. From lap to grass
Whining, motionless on the lowest branch
Above the pine needles, climbing the heather:

We did not listen. It hid there still to find.
Much since was hard to get, later displeased,
Nursing an ordinary complaint or waiting
For a reiterated brilliance,
Growing in ignorance, too near to see.

Now in the suburbs windows are on fire,
Pale globes quiver on their dusty strings
And afternoons disperse with mirth of gnome,
The rigid stabbed flamingo pink in the trees,
Split to the touch and walking by the pool.

Now life jerking in its sustained coda
Constricts its furniture and its events.

The frowning bus disappears down the hill
Or slides before the window with its bored
Passengers staring unashamedly in.

Now above the trees the ice-cream's bare
Electric tongue stammers its recitation.
Children run out in the dumb-bell cul-de-sac
To their cold delight, skipping between the turds
Of long-dead dogs, coiled thickly on the stone.

The children learn so quickly. The house stirs.
Swallows leave earlier, apples to be pressed.
Half the sky burns: the other half is dark.
Hair pushing slowly out, generations
Surrounding us with wonder, theirs and ours.

Nothing to give, nothing has been learnt.
The past simply denies the urge for a truce,
Creeping into the egg. When it is time
We can appoint a committee for the feasts,
And for next year's feasts, and the year after.

Locks stick, glass metamorphosed
In leafy caryatids of summer where
Heat packs the panes and fingers tremble in
Tobacco pockets, a tomato sniffed,
Its greenish acid bloom and tiny hairs.

The pain stirs again like a new life
To be unravelled. It had to come to this.
The body is nothing, the body thinks nothing,
The short senses grubbing on their sticks
Feel nothing, the forgotten carioca.

A line moves to the finger end, and curls,
Head fallen in helplessness. The wails
Of children break behind the woven fences,
Those minted faces far beyond our sight.
The gates shut: a parade of Japanese flags.

And alive on the porch the councillor lowers his pipe,
Comes down from the dunes a bathroom Arab
Firing off caps, or crouched over shells
Gathered in sodden pumps, the soprano waitress
Bringing hot tea across the evening sand.

The nights come in slowly. Behind a half-curtain
The impossible is completed. A single lamp
Weighs down its ornaments in pools of light.
Shadows crawl over the crater, roped
To the terrain's recoil, roped to the pit.

from Cannibals and Missionaries (1972)

The Two Sisters

He saw her fingers in the candlelight
Crooked with the needle, poised to break a thread,
Or at her temple pressed to ease the sight,
With one thin strand of hair loose from her head
Falling in its tiredness, cedar red,
Across the bent and pale half-humorous face,
Hair like a precious garment of the dead
Tucked now behind the ear into its place,
An automatic gesture yet with grace
To make a ceremony of her task
When fingers smoothing down the finished lace
Are answered by the question that they ask
Of labour's quiet satisfaction, such
As simply sanctifies the sight and touch.

That one he loved, the other in a dream
Possessed his spirit, though she never smiled;
One with rolled sleeves or lost in linen's steam,
Fruit in her apron for the orphaned child,
The other walking by herself, beguiled
By passing beggars and by horoscopes;
That home to him, this every day more wild;
One was his shelter, one played out his hopes,
A mind that grasps uncertainty and gropes
For wind-wide vistas from delirious rocks
While others go no further than the slopes
On which they tend the necessary flocks.
Both sisters were his world. From each he learned
What man must die from. And to both returned.

Her sister wasn't helpful, that was certain,
Lying with headaches on her bed all day,
The neighbours wondering at the fastened curtain,
At the strange girl who only knelt to pray
With steps to scrub and the day's fires to lay,
Who stared at breakfast, had no time to spend
In gutting fish and could not see her way
To lay the table for her brother's friend.
The world would take more than one life to mend,
The other thought: there simply wasn't time
To moon about the inevitable end,
For death remained as private as a crime
And as improbable, so long as life
Whitened her knuckles that enclosed the knife.

They told her not to think about the fish.
The fish was simply something they could eat.
It had to die to turn into a dish.
Once dead there was no memory in meat.
She bit her lip, muttered and left her seat,
Her plate untouched. Apologies were made,
A mention of her efforts and the heat:
No wonder nerves were just a little frayed.
But who foresaw as she did death's curved blade
Casting its shadow on the company
And their autumnal guest whose hands displayed
The future's frightening leap, his ruined tree?
Her brother lost to him, white as a sheet,
Her sister still, devoted, at his feet.

And now as if a promise were fulfilled,
Insistently, uncruel, even with joy,
As children tread the towers that they build
And love the crouching cat that they annoy,

Death with his conjuror's fingers took the boy
And left his body still, as one might leave
Forgotten in its box a broken toy.
Mourning has very little to achieve:
A neighbour wiped his eye upon his sleeve
And friends came to console them for their loss.
The sisters found that they could better grieve
If death were seen as swaddling pinned across
His face. They moved their fingers to the brooch
That held it there. Their hope was a reproach.

Death was the knowledge that eluded him,
The senses stunned to feel the body cease,
The spirit sobbing in the missing limb,
The sisters exiled from their brother's lease
And its reversion. In the perfumed peace
Of living's shadow nothing was revealed.
He realized the strangeness would increase
As time unwound its laps about the field
Where he pursued again the power that healed
Its stubborn strokes: those hands laid on his death
Were lent themselves to death and so unsealed
At once his own and every stifled breath
To speak, amazed, of what life was about.
And turn the everlasting inside out.

He was still alive. And the sisters passed
Silently and with great joy into
The landscape of his unbound eyes at last.
One in the wisdom of her insight knew
How life describes its need to be thought true
In terms of its illusions, and she made
Her happiness the air to which she grew.
The other was content to live in shade,

Grew downwards, desperately, undisplayed
Both were his nature. That he understood.
Perhaps uncertain, even half-afraid
Which to embrace, he knew that both were good
As on his heel, beneath his wrinkled skull,
Moved the creased sweating happy miracle.

So when the perfume filled the house she smiled
Inside herself. It was the good part. Both
Were good. She was excited as a child
Though busy with preparing food and loath
To leave it. Someone present swore an oath
It would have paid a labourer for a year,
But who could measure growing against growth,
Or time the seed against the waving ear?
And now one knew it, what was death to fear
But this extraordinary ritual where
Its moment was acknowledged to be near,
Its mystery by a sister's healing hair
Divulged? To smile was to betray her sense
Of love in perfume, tears, experience.

God Bless America

When they confess that they have lost the penial bone and
   outer space is
Once again a numinous void, when they're kept out of
   Other Places,
And Dr Fieser falls asleep at last and dreams of unburnt
   faces,
When gold medals are won by the ton for forgetting about
   the different races,
                              God Bless America.

When in the Latin shanties the scented priesthood suffers
   metempsychosis
And with an organ entry *tutti copula* the dollar uncrosses
Itself and abdicates, when the Pax Americana cuts its losses
And a Pinkville memorial's built in furious shame by
   Saigon's puppet bosses,
                              God Bless America.

When they can be happy without noise, without knowing
   where on earth they've been,
When they cease to be intellectual tourists and stop wanting
   to be clean,
When they send their children to bed at the proper time and
   say just what they mean,
And no longer trust the Quarterly Symposium and the
   Vicarious Screen,
                              God Bless America.

When they feel thoroughly desolated by the short-haired
   Christ they pray to,
When they weep over their plunder of Europe stone by
   stone, releasing Plato

And other Freshman Great Books, when they switch off
    their Hoover and unplug Nato,
Pulling the chain on the CIA and awarding *Time* a rotten
    potato,

                              God Bless America.

When qua-birds, quickhatches and quinnets agree at last
    to admit the quail,
When Captain Queeg is seen descending from the bridge
    as small and pale
As everyone else, and is helped with sympathetic murmurs
    to the rail,
When the few true defenders of love and justice survive to
    tell the tale,

                  Then, perhaps then, God Bless America.

JOHN FULLER

The Choir Master

Alkman, Seventh Century B.C.

Oh my sweet girls, dear girls, with your so clear round
    voices
Linked in the sounds I taught you, your eyes on the page
And all the air no Siren struck with such compulsion
Alive in my ear like the breath of our own Kalliope
Without whose favour dance is graceless, no song moving,
Whose name is always on my lips, and is your name
My dears, as I urge you on like horses to your goal.

Now my legs fail me, standing in the colonnade
Clutching my black heart. If only I could be a bird!
An unharmed gazed-at bird, the colour of distant water,
A bird not alone but flying in easy neighbourhood,
A noble cormorant or tilted migrant gull,
Each far wave bursting for a moment into flower,
Oh my singing pupils, flowers of the sea's same song!

I am old. Your hands slip into mine for friendship
And you sing of the new life, all that I cannot teach.
For there are three seasons: summer and winter, and
    autumn is three,
But in the new life when buds come there is no satisfaction,
Fruit and harvest, none, and no store. Spring is an ache.
In spring the mountains break down and weep, the
    snowdrop
Turns away, heavy with grief. And I clutch my heart,

My heart which is like spring lightning in the mountains
    when
A lantern is dashed to the ground and the gods roar with
    laughter.

In my dream I am rooted and a witness, amazed and
  curious:
They bring a simple dairy churn, though cast in gold,
And you, my dears, fill it yourselves with the milk of a
  lioness!
And proceed to turn out a monstrous cheese which Hermes
  himself
Might well have had appetite for after he'd murdered
  Argos!

Ah well, my own tastes are simple enough. Something
  like porridge
Suits me now. You I've groomed and coaxed, my dear
  sisters,
It's no wonder your skills and beauty astound me still,
As hooves, as wings. You think me an old owl chunnering
In an attic, perhaps, or dare I hope as a ship's pilot
As we steer with one voice like a swan on the streams of
  Xanthus,
Oh my dear girls, Kalliope's daughters, my daughters,
  my music.

Scenario for a Walk-on Part

The borrowed walking-stick that makes me lame,
The single curiously worn-down tyre,
The hanging button and forgotten name,
The grinning of the vulnerable liar:
These are the gambits of a chosen game,
A well-cut personality on hire,
Mirrors too low, the eyebrows graze the frame,
Warming my hands before an unlit fire.

Dinner a skirmish, legs uncrossed and crossed,
An alp of linen and the sight of nylons,
Pudding arriving full of fruit and frost,
And, swimming in their syrup, smoking islands,
Lips at a silver spoon proclaim me lost,
My single joke counters a threat of violence.
The table cleared, I cannot count the cost
Of dinner or of nerves. The rest is silence.

Now in the sharpest lock at close of day,
Hands as if manacled, the gravel spurting,
My hosts with linked arms waving me away,
The gulf of what I didn't say still hurting
(Since you are only known by what you say),
Yawning beneath my silent murmur skirting
The dangerous excuse, the wish to stay,
Like the evasions of protracted flirting:

Alone I drive away with my awareness
That once again I've failed the magic word
Whose demon locks me up inside my bareness,
The charming openness unsaid, unheard.

Is love the better for its hurts and rareness?
I frown and think so. Falling into third
On a hill, I glimpse a face: the sheer unfairness
Fights with my sense of shame at being stirred.

The sexy minister reclaims his scarf,
A girl in denim runs to meet a train,
Mrs Jocasta bastes the fatted calf,
The guests have taken to their beds again:
I hold the floor but nobody will laugh,
No one is there to kiss if I complain,
I enter only in the second half,
Unwilling, underwritten, used to pain.

Aberporth

Sky is performing feats of weather over
Hills wooded to the top, humped private hills
Whose birds look down not up. Briar's between
The fields: he keeps the eating sheep from knowing
What's on the other side. Beneath the path
A culvert runs, hidden for fifty years:
Some work will dig it up again.

Yes, nature is incurious, we know.
The butterflies as big as prayerbooks draw
No lesson from the india wings they thumb through,
While chapel slate aches with its uglification
Of primrose and violet, and the gold-black graves
Make even death elaborate and absurd
Like a bad conjuror.

The sea is much visited here, whose colours are cooler
And life uncertain as well it might be in
The earth's tears. Gulls on the sand look sharp.
Without anxiety the jellyfish is hideously still,
And the same could be said of the cliffs where wind carries
The loves of freewheeling crickets across a haze
Of sun-baked blackberries.

But we so easy are still not at our ease:
Such closeness open to us as though to a
Laconic Christ, hands flat to the ears with pity!
How we wish not to judge, wish for the starlight
And its emblems, the foliage globose and witchy,
With sounds coming nearer (Frrr! Frrr!) speaking
Of something that might content us.

Ghost Village

Something takes me away, even from the spotlit
Indian clubs of our small happy government,
The gasp of hope and memory's applause,
In brown rooms, in yellow rooms, in red rooms by the sea,
To the colourless and soundless world we half-remember.

Presaged and annotated by our paltry sobs,
Older than all the lives we know or ever knew,
So sharply critical of the success of matter,
Keeping its own activities a deadly secret,
It is blind and alert as the black eyes of negatives.

Something said somewhere at some time is not enough
To appease its absorbing interest in what we did not mean
To old friends suddenly noticed as they glance up from
    books
With the sort of look which asks nothing because it is not
    worth it,
By the curled sea in rooms we shall half-forget.

Old friends in new rooms, new friends in old rooms:
It sees them come and go, because it is not worth it,
But a path down the valley cracked with grass
Brings us to the ghosts who must be faced,
Who questioned the blind world and would not let it lie.

Ghosts have hunters, but the hunters lose the track,
For the craned neck does not suspect a reply
And the star or the heron is never asked if it requires
To be looked at, by those who glance up from books
When the curtains are drawn back from the evening sky.

Friendless, rootless by choice, they made a home for this
    bay
Where pairs of stone windows were set to frown at the sea
With all the gloomy unconcern of self-absorbed exiles
Whose delineation of the jealousies and dribbled ghylls
Only betrayed their real longing and peculiar laughter.

Did neighbours wonder at the striding, the leaping of
    gates?
Did Squire Tribute, coming from beyond the ridge
Where the harnessed pismire superb in its plumes of dust
Pretended to be a horse on a careless errand,
Judge? Or was it changed, the outside world?

When Mistress Tidings courted Sinful the Silent
And whispers sent sidling three sides of the square
Returned across the gap shocked and delighted,
Was it too much like what had always been known
To make much sense, the inside world?

For we have known that difference as well,
Hands drumming impatiently on green baize
As we listen to the next to last report,
The tank brimming, the wipers running freely,
Set for the coast and the foul pinks of love.

They took the mountain for its broken counterpart.
Steamers visited the creaking pier and the washed gravel
Lay heaped like wheat on the shore of their closed lives.
In front rooms hands were folded on knees. A ticking clock
Enlarged the stone silences, defining a central gravity.

They saw the cow turn her tail into a handle,
Replenishing three or four fields beside a cliff,

And resolved as they walked alone at evening in
  watchchains
To make their lives acceptable to others, their deaths
Only to themselves. And the fields steamed with joy.

Their children were the first to make shy advances,
Wove with fingers, were pinioned, wept, touched,
Cruelly accused the unhappy of being only unhappy,
Talked incessantly of the marriage of headland and valley
And thought of nothing much to say, but learned to read.

Until one day these became themselves the brooding exiles,
The best cap square set or the downed pick at noon,
The mountain unshaped with interjections of dynamite,
Tired of responsibility, dreaming, easily wounded,
Crying out to be, and being, successfully lured by cities.

Nothing is changed, and most of the dancing is still glum
In neighbouring villages where they watch and wait
For the silver band to assemble in the Sunday dusk.
Nothing is changed, when wishes are fulfilled
And again we stare into the boiling centre.

Nothing is changed, but everything will alter
And the blind world exults as we expect it should
Over the first and last, the inside and outside,
The forms and secrets, friends and generations,
Pacts made by ghosts that some of us have tried to love.

So thinking, a tiny swivelling figure in the bay,
Hands in pockets, turning over stones with a holiday foot,
Posed between the unravelling tides and the abandoned
  houses,
Made an uncertain gesture, ceased watching the sea,
And plodded up the hill for company.

JOHN FULLER

Up and Down*

I

This is where it begins:
A cairn marks the place
Where the earth kissed the sky
And became friends.

Thrown up like apophthegms
Of a phlegmatic culture
During some geological
Tedious prologue

They shoulder for position
While offering their profiles
Like notables at a spa
Grouped for the brush.

They have settled into age
With a fear of being alone.
Such gaunt tranquillity,
A herded peace!

You stand at one's feet
A mere nanunculus,
Or whisper at its brow
An imprecation

Which the wind removes,
Whisked into the air
With all your vanity,
A minor annoyance

*This poem has not previously been published in book form.

Not to be compared
With trigonometry,
Telescopes, masts, picnics
Or the puncture of flags.

Or that old enemy
Who at his leisure reduces
Outcrop to random rocking
Impedimenta.

For as you slither down
The mossed escalation
Of shifting lichen-wrapped
Smashed crocks

A vertical wall to your right
Unbelievably still
And staunch to its terrain,
A ruinous piping

You see what brings you down
Fear stroking the scalp:
Not mere height or exposure
Or being alone

But the dawning role of invader
Animated, flushed, hostile,
Conspirator and wrecker,
Almost indecent.

Up there are old mysteries
Much better left alone,
Safer with our structures
Of docile stone.

2

They own everything,
Saddled with foot-thick wool
And a family resemblance
Like the first Marlboroughs.

Inquisitive and alarmed,
Their slit eyes blank
As undone buttonholes,
They circle the cottage.

To them it memorializes
Worlds of purpose and concept
Unhabitable, like
A stone footprint.

How we come in and out
Is certainly a puzzle
For there they are, puzzled,
Whenever we do it.

Grouped on frosty nights
When with a cautious beam
We tread into the black
Their eyes are green.

And on misty mornings
Moving like ancient sofas
On castors over the gravel
They keep their watch.

For the mountain is edible.
Its small geography
Is their prerogative:
Their paths are meals.

They might even admit
To being its parasites,
As they have parasites
Nuzzling richly.

But what of a creature
Who lives not by the grass
But by the hidden stone,
Its skeleton?

Not as the tasteless crag
Or scrambling sideways scree
Whose dangers are well-known
But a shut cave

In which unspeakable acts
Of gregariousness and greed
Or of sheer stupidity
Are hidden from them?

They may, though bewildered,
Secretly guess our kinship,
Nomads to them and less
Aristocratic.

This would certainly account
For their intermittent patience,
Explain why we feel just
A little sheepish.

3

She makes a quick escape
As from a cold cauldron,
Seeping frugally but
In slight panic

Moistening sheer outcrop
With tears of brave joy,
Long legs down the rock,
A flicker of lace.

Just a slip of a girl
But something to be proud of
Elbowing thorn and stones
And growing stronger

Talking at roadsides where
A small declivity
A tumble of clod and pebble
Whitens her falling

Rushing on in excitement
Through a fledgy wood,
Dropping helter-skelter
Flirting with fish

Lingering in pools
Where hardly visible flies
Have just time enough to cast
A static shadow

And moving down the hillside
Through half-flooded meadows
Where thirsty herds make for
The tell-tale hummocks.

Soon her progress is statelier
On the reed-crowded route
Under footpath and bridge
To her dissolution.

We admire this quality
Of drawing out as on
A thread an argument
Of pure persistence

Until diversity
Sinks with delicious freight
The empty tanker of
Our finite voyage.

For see: the ravine holds her
Where sun-worshippers trudge
With all their full baskets
To the earth's lap.

Whereupon she promptly
Disappears, spilled
Out to random skeins
Across the beach

Rejoining, without complaint,
The globe's great cycle
As who would not wish to do
Did we not stop here?

4

For this is what it comes down to:
After repose, erosion.
From grandeur, detonations
And heartless breakdown.

But if this were the way
We died into the earth
Think of the discretion,
Such privacy!

Privacy of worlds
Not wasted but perpetual,
Tons and tons of indifference,
Lightness of heart.

Grain by grain it offers
Little resistance, only
Corporate mass and that
Agreeably wayward.

Wet, it preserves the wraith
Of toes. Dry, it dissolves
The tread to dredged craters
Lodged with beer-cans.

The loose configurations
Of this sterile humus
Are without finitude:
Frankly, a mess.

Its yellowness is false,
A lie to anger the blue
Which hammers arms and fists
In tears against it.

For down there the chiselled specks
Are proud of their lineage:
Crystal, tan, charcoal,
Their colours are sober.

Flushed by the watery beast
They assert their freedom
In voluntary association,
A righteous rebuttal.

Good reason to admire, then,
The ultimate in stone
Neither to be climbed nor hewn,
The body's haven.

For here we face our star
With least speculation,
Here we are revolved
In certainty.

Here warmth is transmitted.
Your idle hand reaches
And grasps a myriad boulders
Of impossible size.

As they bounce off the palm
Like sparks from a welder
Your hand seems invulnerable,
Colossal. Painless.

PETER LEVI

PETER LEVI

from The Gravel Ponds (1960)

The Gravel Ponds

A tightening net
traps all creatures
even the wildest.

Too late
the young cry out,
and the innocent,
who were not wild enough.

Bodies and tears
are useless;
so few years
are helpless;
free creatures are never wild enough.

The noose closes
making the tragic
young the pathetic
in slum clearance houses.

Never, O never in the long distraction
of the heart's inaction,
never will a cry shake
that prison, or wildness wake.

The young were like those swans
which with folded wings

swim on the gravel ponds
on late June evenings:
like doomed stage characters,
pursued murderers
or slum lovers.

The Catalonian Communist

The Catalonian Communist
is dead, or abroad, or doing fine,
with a wife to keep him warm
or an exile magazine,
and the heart's fog-horn, dull in mist,
can bring no living ship to harm.

And those are out of sight or dead
whose bodies bore the terrible rain,
or who in knots of nervous wire
revolved the images of pain,
who when they lived, the slow heart fed
each hungry nerve with streams of fire.

The rough wind smoulders in the skies
trailing new-coloured dews of ashes,
heroic murder's out of fashion,
the uneasy cities burn in flashes,
and death, the general lover, cries
from under street level his passion.

And God and I and Communists
with little intervals of farce
play glove-puppets with schoolmasters
and terrorize the working-class:
the dead with suddenly sweating wrists
cry out for birth. No birth occurs.

On a Theme of Samuel Palmer

We went along in absolute silence:
it was coming on to a dusk of a clear
hot day, there was a harvest smell.
Armfuls of red apples blushed in the shade,
leaves wound in and out enjoying the cool.
Chestnuts were dying. It was the day of the dead.

Inside the woods there was a cave,
and a wise woman as old as a Sibyl
weaving her hands in the flowing air.
She stood three hours under the blossoming tree
bloody with fruit, may trees in flower,
bloody with fruit, loud with prophecy.

In Midwinter

In midwinter a wood was
where the sand-coloured deer ran
through quietness.
It was a marvellous thing
to see those deer running.

Softer than ashes
snow lay all winter where they ran,
and in the wood a holly tree was.
God, it was a marvellous thing
to see the deer running.

Between lime trunks grey or green
branch-headed stags went by
silently trotting.
A holly tree dark and crimson
sprouted at the wood's centre, thick and high
without a whisper, no other berry so fine.

Outside the wood was black midwinter,
over the downs that reared so solemn
wind rushed in gales, and strong here
wrapped around wood and holly fire
(where deer among the close limes ran)
with a storming circle of its thunder.
Under the trees it was a marvellous thing
to see the deer running.

He Met Her

He met her
at the Green Horse
by the Surrey Docks;
Saturday
was the colour of his socks.

So they loved,
but loving
made nothing better –
drowning cats
in an ocean of water.

What more,
what more could there be,
days or nights?
Nothing
to hear or see but dances and sights.

So they loved,
like the aimless air
or like walking
past shut doors
in a never quiet street and talking.

Alcaeic

Out in the deep wood, silence and darkness fall,
down through the wet leaves comes the October mist;
no sound, but only a blackbird scolding,
making the mist and the darkness listen.

from Water Rock and Sand (1962)

Proposals

I can praise no one but the simply wise and good,
whose words like savage conches haunt and ring
in an echoing daemonic solitude
of the suffering and dead.

They fear no horrors worse than what has been,
but purge the images of their age and passion
as if into ridges of a pure and thin green
receding into rain.

And I can praise no mythical creatures,
breast-heavy Pomona or running Faunus,
no innocent monsters with half-human features:
only reason and nature.

But if when God envisioned Adam
some moonlight man with weeping iron scythe
cut down those dreams of corn and of reason,
I praise this swathe and grain.

To My Friends, for Julian

Tonight the big winds are rising,
whose breath will disturb this whole remote
valley, and make the wires ring
high up and down the scale with a hollow note.

Septembral trees sweep their dark masses
across and across, now a river's voice
bellows from far off, now woods release
shrieks of death-longing into a riot of noise.

And even in so quiet a place
winter comes; whose antique face tonight
hangs close, troubles my sleepy ease,
broods among rain and ponderous storm-light.

One turns over an old newspaper,
its yellowing grim rumours of violence,
the slow degrees of murder: I should prefer,
supposing neither capable of defence,

black private water, a leap into suicide,
where hours and seasons ritually move
in a public dark no violent wish can divide
dull-chiming leaden feet from grave to grave.

But that you, my hopeful friends, live on,
each one in his own hermitage or room,
thinking of weed the winter sea bangs down
on a stone beach, sad aftermath of storm.

Future

If ghosts existed there are some men
who could never effectually belong
to a thin as air congregation,
who'd find the trailing end of some bitter
wind's or yew-tree's slanting thunder
(weeping or not) their place to shelter under.

If ghosts exist I shall be one of them,
knowing with love each individual bright
station of any heavenly spirit;
yet never approaching high for long,
but as if the refracted alleys of distance
were the reality of my thin substance.

No one will need to fear contact
with spirits as content as we shall be,
the devoted private friends of humanity;
we being ghosts shall long ago have swallowed
our private lie, our secret disgrace,
and winnowed mind to influences of place.

Political Poem

A dandelion's head erect
howls in the tortured intellect,
a cloud can murder men and press
whole armies into feebleness,
the smell of hyacinth drunk in
is the revolution's origin.

Two crickets creaking in the grass
can freeze the continental mass,
one vixen round her litter curled
can freeze to death an age of the world,
zoo goats on an artificial crag
are the revolutionary flag.

And the fierce puma and the hot ape
pull their own entrails out of shape,
and the young lovers whose sun
is an absolutely perfect one
deliver over seas and lands
to the violent dead with bloody hands.

Style

I have no myth to express this passion,
which knocks the skull, shaking down words.
Which houses nothing but its myth or passion,
not capable of words or of emotion.
And anyway, in time it had to happen,
I can no longer understand for whom
it seemed a possibility of death to be
young, or a multitude of flowers or questions:
each one a myth, a language and a passion.
I have one myth, and an outworn emotion,
not capable of its true language or passion,
or of my true language, of this passion.

For Alasdair

The book I read this morning tells you how
to become a heron in the world of the dead;
I should prefer (it came into my head)
cheerfully shitting robin on his bough

his ripening colour and his tireless throat
to those great flap-wings and solemnity:
you have to walk Novembers through to see
the personal life expressed in his sweet note.

What I want in the world of the dead is leisure,
dying dissolve my numinous discontents
into a place, the gods into elements,
where time, water and air conspire to pleasure.

Things used for pleasure humanize all places,
green vacuous city, castle and riverbank,
the evening bars, station and taxi-rank
inscribe humanity on uninnocent faces,

and lovers walking in the freshening light
let fly and wander their untroubled sense
in an intensity of innocence
– time, air and water, shadow and night.

Or later when the drifting moon surprises
moonlight walkers, the nothing they pursue,
the river-mist, the fields exhaling dew,
where shivering birds sing as the sun rises.

Nothing but human use can glorify
field, mist, air or light,

common possession and the common right,
and the need of growing which the young live by.

In the world of the dead if there were one
I can do without the violet and the rose:
the democratic young are my heroes,
the casual voices, air, rain, sun.

For Julian Going to America

When you arrive in so sad a city
whose strong fingers teach the sun his place,
chant hymns under your breath to liberty,
her amazing stature and her blank face,

reflecting an abstract rage for her honour
in an unreceptive hand, petrific eyes,
(so I, self-prisoned in my resonant hour
set free these lines as music of her cries).

Now to the groaning of murdered Europe close
your ears: they only can condemn
who breathe an indifferent air's brightness, and those
who are not the first person of a poem:

not in hotels, forewarned by horoscopes,
softly treading the intolerable maze,
but lost from arguments and mocked with hopes,
and unprotected by their lovers' ways;

(so I among these wet woods writing
or in this high room on a wind-rocked night
half-vanish into the clear glass of learning,
the dead boy into crisp yellow and white).

O fear for yourself in that city,
for the poet's first person and his pride,
waiting at dusk or later maybe,
throat muffled, hat pulled on one side,

for the eye's confusion and the phoney dream,
the bedside telephone, the waking mist,

the city autumns offering what they seem,
his tears, his sleep, and love his diarist.

As I below bare Longridge stuck with pines
cower from violence, meditate disgrace,
the atrocious echoes and the long designs
of this stiff portrait, my unloving face.

Since love like freedom shows a ruined front,
a tenement house whose windows peer out blind,
distracted from its perfect self by want
of the fatal lover and the reflective mind.

No poet, no free man or lover
who lodges in that distant city
can walk safe by imaginary power
where its death is, or where its ash will be.

from Fresh Water, Sea Water (1966)

et non erit in te odor ignis . . .

In the morning the pier railings are wet,
the boys high-dive into the autumn sea
like salt-washing a deep stain of the sun,
humanity deserts the public beach.
Humanity should have died out in us,
we should be as the stones are, should retire,
retire, retire. New creatures be walking
hand in hand along the edge of the tide.
It could be colder. Tomorrow's children
will couple on the rampart of the cliffs.
My generation is humanity.
The season in the air burning and bright.
I am in love with these few gulls and birds
which have not deserted my generation.

Freedom

This mountain standing in the sun.
Out of the light into the heat
out of the heat into the wind
out of the wind into the sun.
Out of the rock onto the snow
out of the shadow of the rock
onto the rock below the peak,
off the rock into shadow.
Freedom cannot be ended.
Out of the snow onto the grass
out of the grass onto the face
out of the grass onto the snow.
Freedom cannot be ended.
Out of the cold into the light
out of the heat into the snow
out of the snow onto the grass
and off the grass into the trees
among the trees in the shadow
out of the trees onto the rock.
This mountain standing in the sun.

The Revolutionary in the Public Park

Three rough-eyed dahlias sting the air like flies.
Thin and wet through and starved of nicotine
the empty hedges wake up shivering.
Melodious birds are in the dripping trees.

And we could outface winter in this mood,
my eyes burn petrol like a steel machine.
I write my name in heaven like one line,
heaven falling apart, snow in the road.

If there are not enough of us this year,
yet I believe that we can never lose
running like time for ever I suppose
breathing as sharp as trees, staining the air.

Tractor

Driving the solid field about sunset,
under a wood half picked out in colour,
I fume coarsely along in the fine air,
thinking how mother earth keeps us at it,
swathed in her withering rose and violet,
her thin liquids, her cold and lasting fire.

Everywhere the same lines show,
tree, cloud, furrow and sky overhead
rounded with seed, leaden as an eyelid,
and everything they promise will come true,
a sky so blue it makes rock look blue,
a wood so green it hides the glittering seed.

The earth knows how to breed and to feed us,
her raw juices are still running at least,
the tractor mumbling at its throatiest
speaks to earth in a kind of lover's voice.
All day like larks we rattle around loose
but twilight finds us fumbling with the breast.

Maker and speaker and machine,
and everything said, everything done
gurgles its gritty pap at this season.
More birds make music than can be seen,
dissolving their sweet names in acid green.
The same heat works on everyone.

I want words whose existence is this,
the rough soil and the root work in them,

praising heaven I ever took for theme
this planet, its unnatural wishes,
common reason and human justice,
and growth of life, the last increase of time.

Poem for Julian

Look out into the snow across the park,
day after day, melancholy beauty,
my poetry will be what it can be,
I take some comfort from the early dark.

As harsh as snow my life is in this room,
and thin and green and tough as a poem,
I write it out often thinking of them,
human poets in whom hope was at home.

Here in the room my speckled orchid heaves
its buds half open, brown-gilt and cream-white,
elaborately floating on the light
out of a thick crop of unbarbered leaves.

Human life could have been as cold as this,
and perfect like heaven, never the same,
flower and leaf by leaf, unwritten name,
some mortal poem as this poem is,

but that humanity is just, discovers
a star dying among the fresh planets,
a darkness in which snow falls and forgets,
covering lovers with the names of lovers.

The Poem to Its Master

When you were young I flowed upstairs like water
or stood still like an alcoholic drink,
you had never mastered calligraphy
when I ran on your fingers worse than ink.

When you are old you will not be unhappy,
I shall be the element you forget,
time is tolerant of repetitions
the fresh wording and the fresh cigarette.

When you were young I was unmusical,
I drove you in long cars with canvas hoods
or you were rear-gunner, there was no pilot,
and it was me you shot at in the woods.

Thirty Ways of Drowning in the Sea

1

The surf breaks. Is never silent.
The wind catches the breathing of the surf,
or catches in the breathing of the surf.
The surf hangs in the hearing of the wind
and is not heard.
The wind is never silent.

2

The sea is deep.
Long columns of a green and salty light
Trail downwards, finger for a floor,
disappear in the sand-coloured water.
I am below them in that deep current
a trailing hand of light will never reach.
Among whose grooves and wards the heavy sea
shifts without turning, like a rusted key.

3

This shadow and this light are in the sea
as massive as the mountains in the air.
What is so black as sea?
What is so black as an underwater mountain
lit only by the stars?
This shadow and this light live in the sea.

4

There is always somewhere the sheer breakdown of a
wave at the foot of a cliff. It takes place somewhere,
the whirls of weed of wood and of wildfire,
the anemone and gravel in the undertow,
somewhere there is the heaving vast and empty
but motionable volume of the sea.

5

Marine glitter,
partly blue, partly green,
and a small, hard smell of marine wrack,
a light taste of pickle.

6

A gull has oiled feathers.
Seeing one, he said
'They are the company a sailor has.'
They are infrequent, I suppose he meant.

7

The sea is a mouthing mythology,
should be held in with mouths of jingling harness,
foams, rolls its eye, flings back its head,
it spreads loose shoulders,
it scatters sand and foam, ungovernable.

8

The sea is breathing. The sea is barren breathing.
The breath of sea is sharper in moonlight.
The breath of sea is not a barren nature.
It is an atmosphere. It is a nature
denser than human life can tolerate.

9

In one season the migratory geese
can paint their breast in pink or in purple,
in vaporous snow-dew, or in sea-spray,
be dusted with the soot of the dead moon,
or crumbs of burning stars or shreds of rain,
repeating in their motion a lost meaning
from the expanses of the moving sea.

10

When I was an adolescent
we walked on every landslide and cliff-top
as if they were an old married woman,
hoarded imagination of gunfire,
stood on breakwaters, had an eye for the sea,
which was extreme and utterly silent,
a mesh of light and mess of foam also,
but magnetic and angry without words.

11

They lie and bake on a rock
Dusted with metal water round the rock
takes on a deeper colour from the sun.
There should have been a hero:
a girl out of the sea, blowing a shell,
the crab, the oyster and the coelocanth,
frutti del mare, dusk underwater.
The empty water ripens in the heat
from bright ink-blue to deeper indigo.
There must have been a hero deeper down.

12

The sea at night in winter.
Colder than black.
Bitterly cold and black.
Water crashes and air roars,
pebbles crumble, the mist reverberates.

13

The young brood of a gull can be skewbald,
the sea also can be light brown and white,
piebald or blue and white or green and white;

when the young gull is tired of the wild air
he drops, settles, rides the sea-water;
what choice was brooded in them if the air
is wilder but the sea more violent?

14

In the end a thing will come to the sea,
granitic refuse, dung of a snow-leopard,
ice, or whatever water can carry,
and tree and house together corroded
by greenery, dying of snow-water,
the dune-grass, the river pebble, the coin
will end in the sea, end in the tide.

15

The intense monotony of the noises,
the ungoverned boom, the loose music,
the toot toot of the isolated bird
cover a nature to be reckoned with,
cold, deaf and barbarous,
in habit rougher than will ever sleep,
calamitous the ultimate applause.

16

Dawn smoking and flaming in the dark.
Disintegrated. But the hussar waves
mimic the angry gunfire of the dawn;
the sea is muffled but is resonant,
I think the whole sea is one thudding thing,
one pure chaos of brinish violence
in whose salt spray the wounded men go down
in ragged water, under firing guns.

17

Over the disused acres of the sea
the wind trolls a bladder of black rain
and my poem is sunk in deep water
under the disused acres of the sea.

18

The diving girl and the diving boy
are deep: blue filters of the sun
fall more coldly than the dark.
These children are utterly naked.
The girl has fish eyes open, his are shut,
she has a flowing tail, his is seaweed,
they turn and turn and turn unquietly,
half shadowlike, half alight in the sea.

19

First morning out
we took on board a shoal of bright herring,
unminted silver wealthy in the net.
That night a gale started,
a living wind, it blew two days,
nothing could have stood up,
till on the fourth morning the sea itself
was wrecked, and we were there in the small boats.

20

And yet the sea is not monotonous.
Hungry-bellied, raucous maturity
will drench heaven, will drown the hemisphere,
and will be tame, but will not be computed.
Monotony, Oh perfect intervals
of music, but they are not in the sea.
The sea is brutish and has no music.

21

There was a hermit in a wild sea-cliff
whose voice was harsh with holy canticles,
who fed on terns' eggs and on whin-bushes,
his dying spirit fled into the sea. . . .

22

Throw roses in seawater,
crimson freaked with white or green-eyed white,
throw in weighted bushes of ramblers:
they drown dark green or black.
And let them rot where there are no weeds,
brine and the pure air consume them.

23

The undulations of the wind
increasing in the dark moons of midwinter,
the sea roughens, is empty at that time,
disturbed in its whole depth.
All that roaring and not one word spoken.
Waves insist, insist.
Turmoil is voiceless.

24

Flowers are growing under the pinetree,
light or deep they burn darker in the shade:
the wind is sucking at a lemon-skin.
Out at sea many horizons
heave and glitter in their ranks.
Heat. Light. Nature.
Horizon beyond horizon
biting the eyelids like a need to sleep.
We do not understand what we live by;
the sea's cold body is my life I think,
but I have never felt it in a dream.

25

Now I am caught,
leg, arm, hands and feet,
tugged around in the rough net of the sea,
under cold water like a ton of sand.
The squalling air and the black, wild sea
are eating down the stars of midwinter,
death is caught in the howl of the sea-race.
Dead suns are burning in salt water.
Salt water burns my throat like alcohol.
When shall my body from this death forever
wake with the lash of water in my eyes?

26

The sea stood under a wall of fog,
there was a groundmist in the sea-gardens,
christmas was fumbling with the window panes.
Sea is stark. The sea was stark.
My cat or hyacinth or cyclamen
stewed to death in the quiet lamplight.
The fog hung in the lines of dripping trees.
Sea rises, lamps drown in their light, and we
must suffer the full fury of the sea.

27

The air is full of mist. The mist is full of sun.
The sea is silent.
Everything has been silent all day.
The old year, the old fire
has been drowned into the fire-eating sea;
nothing but the ground-swell can stomach it.
The sea is shameless, it can be silent.
The new year is this small fire in the skies,
gasping down through the mist's infinities.

28

The polished miserere dies away.
Here the deep sea is moving between rocks,
fretting itself to marble-paper foam;
deadly as chemistry, and green as tea,
it swirls underfoot at the cliff-base.
But the first sight of the sea
is distant, hanging high up in the air
biting a long horizon from the sky.

29

Capable hands or hard, bare feet.
The Strawberry, the Saint Demetrius,
and the Canary and the Young Lion
put out to sea. The weather is deserted.
I am thinking of the ugliest of stars
half-drowned in night, washed up by bad weather:
they will come back to anchor like that one.
I speak to it. It is not satisfied.
My fatal light is jangling like a chain.
My fatal light is swinging like a chain,
and at the first moments of a morning
the sea catches rough silver from that star.

30

The waves rumble clearly,
harsh and deep they swallow their humours.
Gladiators are wading round and round
in blood and sand a muddle in the sky.
The sea is beginning to die.
Sea promontories beat their wings of rock
making the spray fly high from the whipped waves,
the long beaches withdraw in their dark mist,

echo by echo picks out the retreat.
The incessant boom boom gathers volume.
Wherever I move I am in the waves.
The sea is in my ears and in my eyes.

from Pancakes for the
Queen of Babylon (1968)

VIII

A city built in darkness and cold air

        cold fire

the cold rattle of sparrows and milk-bottles
and early feet already in the street

Towering tomorrows
wade ankle-deep in a groundmist of gardens.

in any man in his life in the meditation of his heart

        your body, my body

There are five pure colours
and one impure religion.

Darkness.
Far away the mountains are snow-speckled.
The shadow edges forward,
it marks the giant doors of the bus station.

    Dressed in blue canvas the nightwind disperses a smell of
rain of diesels and of sleep. This flurry is colder than the last.

wrapped in a heavy coat my younger brother
vanishes quickly in the smoking fog.

This city is a matter of darkness.

uncertain if my brother ever sleeps
what my life is or does what my life is

Fumes of a dying nest of newspapers,
upstairs alone in an abandoned house.

at other times
when the horsechestnuts lighted their candles

clamour of metal in the snow and mist.

their bodies are like water their life summer,
the sunlight will be rumpling everything

We have come back.

Handfuls of leaves are painting a whole street.

                              and in the nettles where
alleys of shadows and humidity
step downward into ranker water-scenes

The stone itself is
the stones are beginning.

The trees have broken into their new youth.
Houses overhanging rivers
                              suddenly
break out into

Ragged red banners are appearing.

    Your body and my body.

Last week, at the railway station,
you said. Do you remember.
There was a kind of smoky smell of sun.
For us, to whom nothing has been promised.

I can believe in nothing but in God.

my life is in this belief

my life is in this city

X

Thousand on thousand spirits in the sun

    I am at the beginning

the blushing birthday roses in my garden

I cannot keep proverbs out of my voice

guttering in the deeper, deeper air

white the sandflowers sprouting among rocks
whose heavy smell is virgin in the rocks

I cannot keep my life out of my voice

one came back from the Asiatic dead
dragging a mass of Asian foliage:
and those with white faces
who rose early, who soberly rehearsed
some few words that had broken greater sleep.

Storm-clouds were cannonading in mid-air.

horses through the mist
                        serpents in the dust

We have drunk dry the voices in the well.

wild fruit
          fresh water
                   those long-legged boys
the nightstick of the sun will batter down
shouting and swearing, stonily

But underfoot some kind of new grass with a dusky
    breath.
Moisture, whole threads of aubergines. Yellow and purple,
  ripe, ripening.

Or a handful of sparrows at daybreak
coupled again in the rusty scaffolding
break down at night to iron and to stone
the wireless we heard crying in the sun

children's games, lovers' mutterings.

    This spirit was in me.

    I will live in the wind

one who said:
I will eat herbs in the meadows of Glaukos
and live among the dead under the sea,
will feed on honey-cakes and sea-berries,
death and the sea shall herd me with his conch.

Hooters rebounded from Mount Pelion.

Caves will crack and the sea fly apart.

The universe has once been magical

a grain of sugar for the kettle

one who came back
naked under his bronze and linen
his face scarred by planets

this freedom is my theme

green and white comet-tails of fire and ice
trailing into extinction in his eyes

the foxes running on the dead terrace

Daybreak has washed away the dog's print from the dew
these letters from the sand

and shall arise

the second death is deeper than my life

and shall arise
and the moist ringing of a bird-whistle
alleluiando in the blackened trees

and shall arise
This freedom is my theme.

from Life Is a Platform (1971)

This spasm when I write

This spasm when I write and the disorder of my dreams,
this *tremor cordis* in the newspapers, wordy extremes,
all these bell-tones and noises chime the age away,
and God will make them come true in the street one day.
There is heaven in the destruction of this star,
and some philosophy where peace and pleasure are.
I say in the kingdom of the blind music is king
but liberty, reason and life have the most meaning.
Eighteen forty eight and nineteen fourteen
have blotted out democracy as if it had never been.
I say we shall see that generation again.
And God shall fulfil this with his amen.

The break of day . . .

The break of day and the falling of night
birds fish moths in their generations
come without date: there is no infinite:
sea, rock and fossil are my creations.

Poetry without time is a sun-flame
flickering on the misty sea-surface
conversation has always been the same,
seen naked its body has strength and grace:

and I consider I have no future
but sea-blasted roses and foreshore grass,
the strongest languages are most impure,
I wear love on my chest like a horse-brass.

O unwritten poem, secret mountain
peaks, bogmyrtle, bracken and idle men,
handfuls of birds in handfuls of rain,
repeat these words once and forget them then.

Snowy wars . . .

Snowy wars, snow-muffled fruit trees,
a clear moment, a long, bellowing train:
this coughing on the platform, this cognac,
the reeds and floods, the city in the rain,
the prison wall, you can never go back.

Say what it was, what were you looking for
in the darkness, in the trees, in the cold?
My brother who has for so long understood
the fruit on the fruit trees and is lost now.
Reading all night you get cold, you get cold.
The Rome express goes screaming through the wood.

They burnt it down in nineteen forty one.
Why is the wind dry and the dawn dry?
Darkness is in my mind; it is his time;
a musty smell where the birds have nested,
green bushes where the birds will not reply.
The station lamps light you enough really.
Roses have eaten them. This was my crime.

For Joan and Paddy

Fifty years ago I might have died.
Nothing is growing in the villages
but scraggy wheat: *ploutos* repurified.
The children are in leaf darker than trees.
I think there are bare voices in the stars.
The mutterings of those cold fires are wars.

Something died and has come alive in us,
it withers cobble stones and old railings;
beautiful poverty was victorious,
I am fighting the coherence of things.
All my true-seeming words will shake to pieces
when my lamp dies and the dawn cold increases.

Labouring all night on the moon's dark side
I built an iron train: that train is full;
but might have died where Agamemnon died
slowly threshing the water like a gull,
and am in love with cuttings in the rock
where the muse cuckoos like a cuckoo clock.

I have built nothing in thirty-five years
except five wooden gates into a wood.
I sweated mist, beach pebbles were my tears,
red and white dawns which I have understood
broke into cold, and dried up in the end.
The people have no flag left to defend.

There is nothing in providence but leaves,
there is nothing in my heaven but stone;
no one in mountain villages believes
what I believe when I am alone;

the hammer strikes again and again,
it is the gold and silver age again.

Men are like birds and have their building times,
a man's wing will be free and his cheek red,
birds in his hand, not anything that rhymes,
sparkshowers shadows metal compacted,
a note so true that not one bird can sound it
but whole ages of years stand still around it.

A Lost Summer

And a lost summer at a dying point
woods enough hills enough and words enough:
weeds, the dank humus and one eye of light.
Trees and words look loosely. They were not meant.
What is not loose and cannot speak is love.

Out in the miles long looking fields of grain
one tanned roebuck as dark as a raincloud
running like death, freedom is untrodden,
the ragged trees are a dark battle-line
gunning the tattered air over the road.

There is still something in the exhausted soil
clean of association, will break clear
like a late river cloudier than steel
where avenues of leaves coil and uncoil,
like night grass, and fireworms as cold as fear.

What is not loose and cannot speak is love.
Not what she is but she is what they are.
I will be the mad hermit of these woods,
life is a coarse language, it shall be love,
I say nothing shall speak but what they are.

Nothing has been written ...

Nothing has been written about this life.
I am a glacier, I am a rose
as blonde as honey smells of narcissus,
cattle-eyed, the skin dusty but not rough;
white trees are mysteries, the wood is life.

I can tell you this whole wood is bare trees:
what you can smell is the greenness of must
and a white solid blanket of ground-mist,
heavy sleep is the best I can advise
then become wooden-breasted like the trees.

This bible hermit has his kind of life:
his reward is to live thirty years wild
crouching in grass like a hare in a field;
trickles of rain give him water enough,
the truth of his bible is in his life.

Kapetan Michalis

He has gone, leaving written papers.
To many houses, all stone and sky,
some green growth in summer, some deep snow in spring.
Thousands of words of dream scribbled on a bedsheet.
This man tore down the fruit from solitude unripe.

In these woods, in the first leaf of the elm
when stone becomes shadow
the most tormented mind is motionable
it will be stony,
can settle among trees like an enormous butterfly
and shadow becomes stone.

Has gone away through the woods.
Where you hear birds now and then.
Small bodies, shrill voices,
a hundred juliets in balconies of branches.
Indoors at night the yellow globe
illuminating nothing.
Words written in the light of death.
It measures time, ripens without falling.
By now has gone a long way through the woods.

He is above the snowline,
in yellow and white clouds swirling marble
coughed out a star a tiny speck of blood.
You cannot know. You only know that he went on.
Am in this poem like a monastery
inscribing words on air and on darkness,
with the texture of rocks and villages
and the sea's unripeness.

Which is neither mine nor his, but in common.

For Joan

I imagine where God has never been
and a landscape Adam has never seen,
say a broad estuary
crabapple salty on the crooked bough
different from the places we live now;

and I imagine by that estuary
and grape colours and long tones of the sea
quite a new kind of poem
without excuses: thistle, sand and reed
are their own explanation like the creed.

Inland birds cannot enter the poem,
because they carry an intense light with them,
streams of old-fashioned skies;
and half human bird-noises will not fit:
night falls heavy, seabirds understand it.

News

The stain is in my liver and my brains
and my strength is a carcase of soupbones.
Heaven is swirling like a summer cloud,
there is no salt in the weak taste of blood,
the spirit blows to tatters in thin trees
and whines and cannot reach the provinces.
The angry mewing of the party chief
sours the bloodbath by indicating if.
He will become paper, become God,
a paper taste alternative to blood.

from Death is a Pulpit (1971)

Letter on the Art of Satire,
to Ned Sherrin

When traffic died I dreamed the other night
about a god with sheepskin wig and tight
violet breeches writing ****, and then
satiric verses with a golden pen.
And God knows what the art of satire is,
I wish I had metallic breath like his,
the only metal in my constitution
is if you talk about a revolution
a knife gets whetted on a stone somewhere
in my stomach and starts to glitter there,
and words for happiness and freedom make
my skull ring like a bell and my ribs shake.
And God knows who's the greatest satirist,
whose the cold anger and the whippy wrist,
who was afraid enough to show contempt,
yet curious in every new attempt,
proud enough to be angry and not weep,
and loud enough to laugh rather than sleep.
Satiric truth, epigrammatic wit,
secret weeping and a hard open hit
became one thing in Alexander Pope,
the gadfly with the midget skipping-rope,
the wild firedrake trailing a wounded wing,
the scorpion dying of his own sting.
Caverns and grottoes raped him in the dark,
his rest a glitter, his whole mind a spark.
Can you awake a new satiric age
without some poet in a hermitage?

The only poet of the age of doubt,
Byron is too far gone to write about,
and the few stinging poets now alive
are wild bees in the rocks without a hive.
Auden has been too clever for too long,
the sirens have drowned Spender in their song,
and the old showman of this dying fair
Eliot has sucked fire out of the air,
and vanished into fire, that fire is gone,
and we have all been charred to skin and bone.
The miners cough and work their vein alone.
Prose can be strong and funny, but the rot
withers that worst, young novelists are not
as absolute as poets ought to be;
God knows what is human integrity.
It is to scrape at heaven and be just,
know the clear diamond in the dead dust,
write what is good not what is innocent,
praise reason but not live by argument,
dive after truth, know nature, fight pretence,
admit we live at one another's expense,
be barbarous, love God and human life,
live where the hawk lives, strike with the sun's knife.
You may be godlike and admired and wise,
if you are not the thing you satirize:
live how you like, only write well, and then
we shall read it, and may die happy men.
Live by a lamplight blacker than the blind,
peer out at night through peepholes at mankind,
use a distorted lens, stare in the sun,
then make your subject a distorted one,
Powell at prayer or Douglas-Home at whist,
and learn from God to be a satirist.
Turn on the Queen's horses and the full heat,

maggots and John Gordon and reasty meat.
But if this sort of stuff should make you sick,
there are three kinds of privileged critic
of whose unreasoned rage you might be glad,
prisoners, and schoolchildren, and the mad.
What those tormented minds see by bat-light
sober satire should settle down to write,
brush reasons off, drive poetry away,
bring raw nightmares prancing out at midday,
tell spirit how it lies, call hope a whore,
purge my stomach with laughter and terror.

ADRIAN MITCHELL

from Poems (1964)

Four for Children

The elephant knocked the ground with a stick,
He knocked it slow, he knocked it quick.
He knocked it till his trunk turned black –
Then the ground turned round and knocked him back.

If I had a rusty concrete mixer
I would fill it with Murcheson's Cough Elixir.
Doesn't the thought of it make you sick, sir?

Lovers lie around in it
Broken glass is found in it
Grass
I like that stuff

Tuna fish get trapped in it
Legs come wrapped in it
Nylon
I like that stuff

Eskimos and tramps chew it
Madame Tussaud gave status to it
Wax
I like that stuff

Elephants get sprayed with it
Scotch is made with it
Water
I like that stuff

Clergy are dumbfounded by it
Bones are surrounded by it
Flesh
I like that stuff

Harps are strung with it
Mattresses are sprung with it
Wire
I like that stuff

Carpenters make cots of it
Undertakers use lots of it
Wood
I like that stuff

Cigarettes are lit by it
Pensioners get happy when they sit by it
Fire
I like that stuff

Dankworth's alto is made of it, most of it,
Scoobdedoo is composed of it
Plastic
I like that stuff

Man made fibres and raw materials
Old rolled gold and breakfast cereals
Platinum linoleum
I like that stuff

Skin on my hands
Hair on my head
Toenails on my feet
And linen on my bed
Well I like that stuff
Yes I like that stuff
The earth
Is made of earth
And I like that stuff

The runaway train knocked the buffers flat:
'Hey,' said the stationmaster, 'that's enough of that.
I've been forty-two years at this station
And I've never seen such bufferation.'

A Child is Singing

A child is singing
And nobody listening
But the child who is singing:

Bulldozers grab the earth and shower it.
The house is on fire.
Gardeners wet the earth and flower it.
The house is on fire,
The houses are on fire.
Fetch the fire engine, the fire engine's on fire.
We will have to hide in a hole.
We will burn slow like coal.
All the people are on fire.

And a child is singing
And nobody listening
But the child who is singing.

The Dust

Singing, as she always must,
Like the kitten-drowner with a howling sack,
Open-eyed through the shallow dust
Goes the dust-coloured girl with a child on her back.

A schoolgirl in a flowered dress,
Swayed by the swaying of a tree
And the sun's grin, in front of her family
One day became a prophetess.

Like a singer who forgets her song
She awkwardly leant from the graceful chair,
Balanced her fists in the drawing-room air
And said that everyone was wrong, that she was wrong.

Shocked by this infantile mistake
Her uncles and aunts were sad to find
This ugly girl with an ugly mind
In a house as rich as birthday cake.

When the bombs fell, she was sitting with her man,
Straight and white in the family pew.
While in her the bud of a child grew
The city crumbled, the deaths began.

Now, singing as she always must,
A refugee from a love burned black,
Open-eyed through the rising dust
Goes the dust-coloured girl with a child on her back.

from Out Loud (1968)

Icarus Shmicarus

If you never spend your money
you know you'll always have some cash.
If you stay cool and never burn
you'll never turn to ash.
If you lick the boots that kick you
then you'll never feel the lash,
and if you crawl along the ground
at least you'll never crash.
So why why why –
WHAT MADE YOU THINK YOU COULD FLY?

To You

One: we were swaddled, ugly-beautiful and drunk on milk.

Two: cuddled in arms always covered by laundered sleeves.

Three: we got sand and water to exercise our imaginative
faculties.

Four: we were hit. Suddenly hit.

Five: we were fed to the educational system limited.

Six: worried by the strange creatures in our heads, we
strangled some of them.

Seven: we graduated in shame.

Eight: World War Two and we hated the Germans as much
as our secret bodies, loved the Americans as much as the
Russians, hated killing, loved killing. depending on the
language in the Bible in the breast pocket of the dead sol-
dier, we were crazy-thirsty for Winston Superman, for
Jesus with his infinite tommy-gun and the holy Spitfires,
while the Jap dwarfs hacked through the undergrowth
of our nightmares – there were pits full of people-meat –
and the real bombs came, but they didn't hit us, my love,
they didn't hit us exactly.

My love, they are trying to drive us mad.

So we got to numbers eight, nine, ten, and eleven,

Growing scales over every part of our bodies,

Especially our eyes,

Because scales were being worn, because scales were
armour.

And now we stand, past thirty, together, madder than ever,

We make a few diamonds and lose them.

We sell our crap by the ton.

My love, they are trying to drive us mad.

Make love. We must make love
Instead of making money.
You know about rejection? Hit. Suddenly hit.
Want to spend my life building poems in which untamed
People and animals walk around freely, lie down freely
Make love freely
In the deep loving carpets, stars circulating in the ceiling,
Poems like honeymoon planetariums.
But our time is burning.
My love, they are trying to drive us mad.

Peace was all I ever wanted.
It was too expensive.
My love, they are trying to drive us mad.

Half the people I love are shrinking.
My love, they are trying to drive us mad.

Half the people I love are exploding.
My love, they are trying to drive us mad.

I am afraid of going mad.

The Liberal Christ Gives an Interview

I would have walked on the water
But I wasn't fully insured.
And the BMA sent a writ my way
With the very first leper I cured.

I would've preached a golden sermon
But I didn't like the look of the Mount.
And I would've fed fifty thousand
But the Press wasn't there to count.

And the businessmen in the temple
Had a team of coppers on the door.
And if I'd spent a year in the desert
I'd have lost my pension for sure.

I would've turned the water into wine
But they weren't giving licenses.
And I would have died and been crucified
But like – you know how it is.

I'm going to shave off my beard
And cut my hair,
Buy myself some bulletproof
Underwear
I'm the Liberal Christ
And I've got no blood to spare.

To Nye Bevan Despite His Change of Heart

Because I loved him
I believe that somebody dropped blood-freezing powder
Into the water-jug of vodka which Nye Bevan swigged
Before he asked us:
Do you want Britain to go naked to the conference table?

A difficult question.
Whoever saw Britain naked?
Britain bathes behind locked doors
Where even the loofah is subject to the Official Secrets Act.
But surely Britain strips for love-making?
Not necessarily.
An analysis of British sexual response
Proves that most of the United Kingdom's acts of love
Have been undertaken unilaterally.
There have been persistently malicious rumours
From Africa and Asia
That Britain's a habitual rapist
But none of the accusers have alleged
That Britain wore anything less than full dress uniform
With a jangle of medals, bash, bash,
During the alleged violations.

So do you want Britain to go naked to the conference
    table?
Britain the mixed infant,
Its mouth sullen as it enters its second millenium
Of pot-training.
Britain driven mad by puberty,
Still wearing the uniform of Lord Baden-Powell
(Who was honoured for his services to sexual mania).
Britain laying muffins at the Cenotaph.

Britain, my native archipelago
Entirely constructed of rice pudding.

So do you want Britain to go naked to the conference table?
Yes. Yes Nye, without any clothes at all.
For underneath the welded Carnaby
Spike-studded dogcollar groincrusher boots,
Blood-coloured combinations
And the golfing socks which stink of Suez,
Underneath the Rolls Royce heart
Worn on a sleeve encrusted with royal snot,
Underneath the military straitjacket
From the Dead Meat Boutique –
    Lives
    A body
Of incredibly green beauty.

For David Mercer

I like dancers who stamp.
Elegance
Is for certain trees, some birds,
Expensive duchesses, expensive whores,
Elegance, it's a small thing
Useful to minor poets and minor footballers.
But big dancers, they stamp and they stamp fast,
Trying to keep their balance on the globe.
Stamp, to make sure the earth's still there,
Stamp, so the earth knows that they're dancing.
Oh the music puffs and bangs along beside them
And the dancers sweat, they like sweating
As the lovely drops slide down their scarlet skin
Or shake off into the air
Like notes of music.
I like dancers, like you, who sweat and stamp
And crack the ceiling when they jump.

Adrian Mitchell's Famous Weak Bladder Blues

Now some praise God because he gave us the bomb to drop
    in 1945
But I thank the Lord for equipping me with the fastest
    cock alive.

You may think a sten-gun's frequent, you can call greased
    lightning fast,
But race them down to the Piccadilly bog and watch me
    zooming past.

    Well it's excuse me,
    And I'll be back.
    Door locked so rat-a-tat-tat.
    You mind if I go first?
    I'm holding this cloudburst.
    I'll be out in 3.7 seconds flat.

I've got the Adamant Trophy, the Niagara Cup, you should
    see me on the M.1 run,
For at every comfort station I've got a reputation for –
    doing the ton.

Once I met that Speedy Gonzales and he was first through
    the door.
But I was unzipped, let rip, zipped again and out before he
    could even draw.

Now God killed Lenny Bruce and he let Bob Hope survive,
But the good Lord blessed little Adrian Mitchell with the
    fastest cock alive.

Peace Is Milk

Peace is milk.
War is acid.
The elephant dreams of bathing in lakes of milk.
Acid blood
Beats through the veins
Of the monstrous, vulture-weight fly,
Shaking, rocking his framework.

The elephants, their gentle thinking shredded
By drugs disseminated in the electricity supply,
Sell their children, buy tickets for the Zoo
And form a dead-eyed queue
Which stretches from the decorative, spiked gates
To the enormous shed where the flies are perching.

Peace is milk
War is acid.
Sometimes an elephant finds a bucket of milk.
Swash! and it's empty.
The fly feeds continually.
The fly bulges with acid
Or he needs more. And more.

An overweight fly levers himself
From his revolving chair,
Paces across the elephantskin floor,
Presses a button
And orders steak, steak, elephant steak
And a pint of acid.

Peace is milk.
War is acid.

The elephants are being dried in the sun
The huge flies overflow.

Look down from the plane.
Those clouds of marvellous milk.
Easily they swing by on the wind,
Assembling, disassembling,
Forming themselves into pleasure-towers,
Unicorns, waterfalls, funny faces;
Swimming, basking, dissolving –
Easily, easily.

Tomorrow the cream-clouds will be fouled.
The sky will be buckshot-full of paratroop swarms
With their money-talking guns,
Headlines carved across their foreheads,
Sophisticated, silent electrical equipment.
Heart-screws and fear-throwers.
The day after tomorrow
The clouds will curdle, the clouds will begin to burn –
Yes, we expected that, knew about that,
Overkill, overburn, multi-megacorpse,
Yeah, yeah, yeah we knew about that
Cry the white-hearted flies.

Channel One –
A fly scientist in an ivory helmet
Who always appears about to cry
Explains why the viewers have to die.

Channel Nine –
A fly statesman,
Hardly audible through the acid rain,
Explains why nothing can ever happen again.

Oh we'll soon be finished with the creatures of the earth.
There's no future in elephants, milk or Asiatics.
We should be working out
How to inflict the maximum pain
On Martians and Venusians.

Sour sky.
The elephants are entering the shed.
Sour sky.
The flies have dropped a star called Wormwood
And turned the Pacific into an acid bath.
Sour sky.
Socrates said no harm could come to a good man,
But even Socrates
Couldn't turn the hemlock into a banana milk-shake
With one high-voltage charge
From his Greek-sky eyes.
Even Socrates, poor bugger.

They are rubbing their forelegs together,
Washing each others holes with their stubbled tongues,
Watching us while they wash.
Then, like brown rain running backwards,
They hurtle upwards, vibrating with acid.
They patrol our ceilings, always looking downwards.
Pick up the phone, that's them buzzing.
The turd-born flies.

Peace is milk
And milk is simple
And milk is hard to make.
It takes clean grass, fed by clean earth, clean air, clean rain,
Takes a calm cow with all her stomachs working
And it takes milk to raise that cow.

The milk is not for the good elephant.
The milk is not for the bad elephant.
But the milk may be for the lucky elephant
Looming along until the end of the kingdom of the flies.

A family of people, trapped in Death Valley,
Drank from the radiator,
Laid out the hubcaps as bowls for the dew,
Buried each other up to the neck in sand
And waited for better times, which came
Just after they stopped hoping.

So the sweet survival of the elephants demands
Vision, cunning, energy and possibly burial
Until, maybe, the good times roll for the first time
And a tidal wave of elephants,
A stampede of milk,
Tornadoes through the capitals of flydom,
Voices flow like milk,
And below the white, nourishing depths –
Bodies moving any way they want to move,
Eyes resting or dancing at will,
Limbs and minds which follow, gladly,
The music of the milk.

So you drink my milk, I'll drink yours.
We'll melt together in the sun
Despite the high-explosive flies
Which hover, which hover,
Which hover, which hover,
Like a million plaguey Jehovahs.

Their prisons, their police, their armies, their laws,
Their camps where Dobermans pace the cadaver of a field,

Their flame factories and Black Death Factories,
The sourness of their sky –
Well that's the poisonous weather the elephants must
    lumber through,
Surviving, surviving,
Until the good times roll for the first time.

But it doesn't end
With an impregnable city carved out of the living light.
It doesn't end
In the plastic arms of an Everest-size Sophia Loren.
It doesn't end
When the world says a relieved farewell to the white man
As he goofs off to colonize the Milky Way.

It continues, it continues.
When all of the elephants push it goes slowly forward.
When they stop pushing it rolls backwards.
It continues, it continues.
Towards milk, towards acid.

The taste of milk has been forgotten.
Most elephants agree peace is impossible.
Choosing death instead, they are jerked towards death
Slowly by newspapers, nightmares or cancer,
More quickly by heroin or war.
And some, the tops of their skulls sliced off
By money-knives or the axes of guilt,
Bow their great heads and let their hurting brains
Slop in the lavatory to drown.

There are prophets – grand-children of William Blake –
Desperate elephants who drink a pint of diamonds.
Their eyes become scored with a thousand white trenches,

Their hide shines with a constellation
Of diamond-headed boils,
Each footstep leaves a pool of diamond dust.
And sure, they shine,
They become shouting stars,
Burning with light until they are changed by pain
Into diamonds for everyone.
And sure, they go down shining,
They shine themselves to death,
The diamond drinkers.

The world is falling to pieces
But some of the pieces taste good.

There are various ways of making peace,
Most of them too childish for English elephants.
Given time and love it's possible
To cultivate a peace-field large enough
For the playing of a child.
It's possible to prepare a meal
And give it with care and love
To someone who takes it with care and love.
These are beginnings, but it's late, late –
TV Dinner tonight.
It's possible to suck the taste of peace
From one blade of grass
Or recognize peace in a can of white paint,
But it's not enough.
In Nirvana there's only room for one at a time.

WELL, YOU COULD STOP KILLING PEOPLE FOR A START

Let loose the elephants.
Let the fountains talk milk.

Free the grass, let it walk wherever it likes.
Let the passports and prisons burn, their smoke turning
    into milk.
Let the pot-smokers blossom into milk-coloured mental
    petals.
We all need to be breast-fed
And start again.

Tear the fly-woven lying suits
Off the backs of the white killers
And let their milky bodies
Make naked pilgrimage
To wash the sores of Africa and Asia
With milk, for milk is peace
And money tastes of guns,
Guns taste of acid.

Make love well, generously, deeply.
There's nothing simpler in the savage world,
Making good love, making good good love.
There's nothing harder in the tender world,
Making good love, making good good love,
And most of the elephants, most of the time
Go starving for good love, not knowing what the pain is,
But it can be done and thank Blake it is done,
Making good love, making good good love.
In houses built of fly-turds, in fly-turd feasting mansions,
Fly-fear insurance offices even,
Fly-worshipping cathedrals even,
Even in murder offices just off the corridors of fly-power —
Making good love, making good good love.

Good lovers float,
Happy to know they are becoming real.
They float out and above the sourness, high on the seeds of
    peace.
There are too few of them up there.
Too little milk.
Drink more milk.
Breed more cows and elephants.
Think more milk and follow your banana.
We need evangelist, door-to-door lovers,
Handing it out, laying it down,
Spreading the elephant seed, delivering the revolutionary
    milk,
Making good love, making good good love.
United Nations teams of roving elephant milkmen
Making good love, making good good love,
Because peace is milk,
Peace is milk
And the skinny, thirsty earth, its face covered with flies,
Screams like a baby.

from Ride the Nightmare (1971)

Vroomph! or The Popular Elastic Waist

Juliet sighs. Romeo speaks.
Deep shelters are out of most people's reach.
The white tin is a simple gadget for pinpointing
    the size and position of nuclear bursts.
Simply push the needle in, pump the handle, and
You haven't seen anything till you've seen
    the 200 pounds of beautiful Louise
Tucked away in the secret, hardened, national seat
    of government,
Or balanced on bicycles while removing 12 shirts.
Yet, even when we made love, at a time when most
    women are feeling romantic, she would start to
        prattle away about
The Royal State Trumpeters of the Household Cavalry.

Stimulated by these breaks in the nuclear overcast,
    the *Sunday Times* here offers what is probably the
        first complete review of our Civil Defence
        preparations,
A symbol of the virile, aggressive, muscular game which
    one associates with a man who has twice broken the
        same leg – and twice returned to the game.
This is the problem: whether to drink Cointreau neat
    and slowly savour every warming sip,
Or hang from the tops of palm trees by our feet.

While we have the bomb it seems ridiculous not to be
    honest.

It works like this: the motor is powered by ordinary
    torch batteries.
The slightly wounded will be sent on their way, the
    severely wounded left to
The Marquis de Ferara.

Fill out the Panic Sheet.
Neither the *Sunday Times* nor its agents accepts any liability
    for loss or
The gruesome electric chair.
You see, we are unashamedly devoted to the kind
    of quiet courtesy
        which gets rarer
            every
                day.

What to Do if You Meet Nijinsky

The special child
Remains a child
Knowing that everything else
Is smaller, meaner and less gentle.

Watch the creature standing
Like a fountain in a photograph.
He's moving carefully as a leaf
Growing in a hothouse.
What are the roots?
What is the stem?
What are the flowers?
Nijinsky
Dancing too much truth.

If you don't kill Nijinsky
He's going to turn you into Nijinsky.
You'll live like a leaf, die like a leaf,
Like Nijinsky.

Sweet magical
Skinned
Alive
Animal

You must decide for yourself how you're going to kill
Nijinsky.

Leave him in the prison
Whose stones are cut so cleverly
They fit every contour of his skin exactly.

Leave him collapsing
In the foreign forest clearing
While the pine trees burn around him like a circle of
matches.

Climb into your car and drive like a rocket right out of the
world of feeling.

Leave Nijinsky dancing
The dance of lying very still.

Open Day at Porton

These bottles are being filled with madness,
A kind of liquid madness concentrate
Which can be drooled across the land
Leaving behind a shuddering human highway . . .

    A welder trying to eat his arm.

    Children pushing stale food into their eyes
    To try to stop the chemical spectaculars
    Pulsating inside their hardening skulls.

    A health visitor throwing herself downstairs,
    Climbing the stairs, throwing herself down again
    Shouting: Take the nails out of my head.

There is no damage to property.

Now, nobody likes manufacturing madness,
But if we didn't make madness in bottles
We wouldn't know how to deal with bottled madness.

We don't know how to deal with bottled madness.

We all really hate manufacturing madness
But if we didn't make madness in bottles
We wouldn't know how to be sane.

Responsible madness experts assure us
Britain would never be the first
To uncork such a global brainquake.

But suppose some foreign nut sprayed Kent
With his insanity aerosol . . .
Well, there's only one answer to madness.

How To Kill Cuba

You must burn the people first,
Then the grass and trees, then the stones.
You must cut the island out of all the maps,
The history books, out of the old newspapers,
Even the newspapers which hated Cuba,
And burn all these, and burn
The paintings, poems and photographs and films
And when you have burnt all these
You must bury the ashes
You must guard the grave
And even then
Cuba will only be dead like Che Guevara –
Technically dead, that's all,
Technically dead.

Please Keep Off the Dead

My Uncle Superhubert joined the Graveyard Police,
Says you couldn't wish for a sweeter manor.

Sometimes they hold a March of the Zombies,
But that's traditional, my Uncle leads them.
Once round the boneyard and back to bed.

He gets the odd villain.
A couple of revolutionaries
Whose graves keep catching on fire
But mostly they're a decent mob, the dead.

Last week my Uncle went down to Gethsemane Corner
And rolled the stone away
And there was Bing Crosby
Singing 'The Bells of St Mary's'.

Just Off Charing Cross Road There Are Alleys Full of Crocodiles

I'm dreaming about the fiscal year,
But I promise you, I promise you –
And I'll sharpen my forefinger to
A red-streaming ballpoint pen
So I can put this promise in writing you'll believe –
I don't want to live with Julie Andrews.

Warming my eyes in a bar.
The man on my left says Safe Deposit.
The lady on my right says Shirt.
Someone else says: You'd Think You'd
Get A Decent Life For A Pound A Head.

ADRIAN MITCHELL

The Oxford Hysteria of English Poetry

Back in the caveman days business was fair.
Used to turn up at Wookey Hole,
Plenty of action down the Hole
Nights when it wasn't raided.
They'd see my bear-gut harp
And the mess at the back of my eyes
And 'Right,' they'd say, 'make poetry,'
So I'd slam away at the three basic chords
And go into the act –
A story about sabre-toothed tigers with a comic hero,
A sexy one with an anti-wife-clubbing twist –
Good progressive stuff mainly,
Get ready for the Bronze Age, all that,
And soon it would be 'Bring out the woad!'
Yeah, woad. We used to get high on woad.

The Vikings only wanted sagas
Full of gigantic deadheads cutting off each other's vitals
Or Beowulf Versus the Bog People.
The Romans weren't much better,
Under all that armour you could tell they were soft
With their central heating
And poets with names like Horace.

Under the Normans the language began to clear,
Became a pleasure to write in,
Yes, write in, by now everyone was starting
To write down poems.
Well, it saved memorizing and improvising
And the peasants couldn't get hold of it.
Soon there were hundreds of us,
Most of us writing under the name
Of Geoffrey Chaucer.

Then suddenly we were knee-deep in sonnets.
Holinshed ran a headline:
BONANZA FOR BARDS.

It got fantastic –
Looning around from the bear-pit to the Globe,
All those freak-outs down the Mermaid,
Kit Marlowe coming on like Richard the Two,
A virgin Queen in a ginger wig
And English poetry in full whatsit –
Bloody fantastic, but I never found any time
To do any writing till Willy finally flipped –
Smoking too much of the special stuff
Sir Walter Raleigh was pushing.

Cromwell's time I spent on cultural committees.

Then Charles the Second swung down from the trees
And it was sexual medley time
And the only verses they wanted
Were epigrams on Chloe's breasts
But I only got published on the back of her left knee-cap.

Next came Pope and Dryden
So I went underground.
Don't mess with the Mafia.

Then suddenly – WOOMF –
It was the Ro-man-tic Re-viv-al
And it didn't matter how you wrote,
All the public wanted was a hairy great image.
Before they'd even print you
You had to smoke opium, die of consumption,
Fall in love with your sister

And drown in the Mediterranean (not at Brighton).
My publisher said: 'I'll have to remainder you
Unless you go and live in a lake or something
Like this bloke Wordsworth.'

After that there were about
A thousand years of Tennyson
Who got so bored with himself
That he changed his name
To Kipling at half time.
Strange that Tennyson should be
Remembered for his poems really,
We always thought of him
As a golfer.

There hasn't been much time
For poetry since the 'twenties
What with leaving the Communist Church
To join the Catholic Party
And explaining why in the C.I.A. Monthly.
Finally I was given the Chair of Comparative Ambiguity
At Armpit University, Java.
It didn't keep me busy,
But it kept me quiet.
It seemed like poetry had been safely tucked up for the
    night.

Involvement

QUESTION (from the *London Magazine*):

In most European countries, and in America, writers are becoming involved, one way or another, in public mani-festations of protest. As an English writer, do you feel that working on your own terms is more important than taking a practical part in organizing public opinion?

In other words, in the continuing debates – about race, class, violence, war, financial priorities – that crucially affect our lives, are you for the writer in any way as polemicist, or do you believe that his instinct as an artist is ultimately the real test of his integrity?

ANSWER:

SCENE: an alley.

(A MAN is being beaten up by TWO SECRET POLICEMEN. An ENGLISH WRITER approaches.)

> MAN
> Help!

> ENGLISH WRITER
> Well, that may be what you think you
> want. But I've got to work on my own
> terms.

> MAN
> Help!

(TWO SECRET POLICEMEN put the boot in.)

ENGLISH WRITER
Look, I don't like this any more than
you do. But I've got to follow my own
instinct as an artist.

MAN (spitting teeth)
Yes, well that's ultimately the real
test of your integrity.

(The beating up continues.
ENGLISH WRITER pisses off to write a poem about
ants.)

CURTAIN

We Call Them Subnormal Children

(from *The Body*)

They are here, they are here,
they are very far away.

Perhaps they see exciting visions
in the hollows of their hands.
Perhaps they can hear music we are deaf to

but I think their hearts trudge
and that their days trudge

for the way they sort of stand
the way they sort of speak

laboriously expresses one word only
wounded wounded wounded

We are taking a deep breath before the long slow dive
    through space to Mars.

We have not yet explored these island people.

They are here.
They will not go away.

21st Century Werewolf

(from *The Hotpot Saga*)

I was zooming round the universe feeling like Desperate
    Dan
I was bombing them at random in the hope of hitting
    Charlie Chan
I looked and saw a continent without a single man
Which they told me was Asia but it looked more like
    Aberfan

Ride the nightmare
Jump upon its hairy back
Ride the nightmare
Ride until your mind goes black
It's the 21st Century Werewolf
And it's coming this way

Well the charity lady wiped the diamonds from her eyes and
    said
I've been saving all my pennies but the African dead stay
    dead
I'm sending them Elastoplast and Dunlopillo bread
But they wrote me a letter saying, Send us guns instead

Ride the nightmare
Jump upon its hairy back
Ride the nightmare
Ride until your mind goes black
It's the 21st Century Werewolf
And it's coming this way.

Well the rich white Englishman can easily ignore the rest
For the poor are just a bore and who can use the starving
   and oppressed?
They're burning while you tell yourself there's nothing you
   can do
When their turn comes they'll do just the same for you

So ride the nightmare
Jump upon its hairy back
Ride the nightmare
Ride until your mind goes black
It's the 21st Century Werewolf
And it's coming this way.

ADRIAN MITCHELL

Byron Is One of the Dancers

His poems – they were glad with jokes, trumpets,
   arguments and flying crockery
                 Rejoice
He shook hearts with his lust and nonsense, he was
   independent as the weather
                 Rejoice
Alive, alive, fully as alive as us, he used his life and let life
   use him
                 Rejoice
He loved freedom, he loved Greece, and yes of course, he
   died for the freedom of Greece
                 Rejoice

    And yes, this is a dance,
    and yes, beyond the glum farrago
    of TV cops after TV crooks
    in the blockheaded prison of TV –

    I hear the naked feet of Byron
    which skated once, powered by fascination
    over the cheerful skin of women's legs,
    I hear those two bare feet –
    One delicate and one shaped horribly –
    slap and thud, slap, thud, slap, thud,
    across the cracked-up earth of Greece,
    and yes, I hear the music which drives those feet
    and feel the arm of Byron round my shoulder
    or maybe it is round your shoulder
    Oh I feel your arm around my shoulder
    and yes, I know the line of dancers
    across the cracked-up earth of Greece
    stretches from sea to sea

as the shrivelled mountains erupt into music
and Byron and all the million dancers
yes brothers and sisters, lovers and lovers,
some lucky in life and delicately-skinned,
some shaped horribly by want or torture,
dance out the dance which must be danced
for the freedom of Greece
for the freedom of Greece

Dance
Rejoice
Dance
Rejoice

ADRIAN MITCHELL

Loose Leaf Poem

(This is a diary of good and bad things, mostly for friends
and allies but with a few sections for enemies as well. It was
written in a peaceful room with a view of the Yorkshire
Dales. In reading it aloud, I often change the order of
sections, talk in between sections and leave out any part
which doesn't seem relevant at the time.)

There was a child danced with a child
The music stopped

*   *   *

I stopped reading *The Wretched of the Earth*
Because you cannot read it all the time.

My stomach felt like outer space.
The sunday papers all sounded
Like bidders in a slave market.

I ate rapidly, alone,
Because I couldn't sit and eat with anyone,
Or look at anyone.

I glanced into the television's eye.
It was both bright and blind.

I was full of useless tears.
I did not use them.

*   *   *

Who was the hooligan who ripped off all your skin,
   madam?

The North Atlantic Treaty Organization.

*　　　*　　　*

Below my window, a stone wall begins,
swerves past a tree, drags its weight
upwards, almost collides with a second tree,
breaks for a gate, resumes,
and skitters over the horizon.
I watch the way it rides,
blonde stone in the blonde light of Yorkshire.

*　　　*　　　*

Are you bored by pictures of burning people?
You will be bored to death.

They did the dying.
You did nothing.

Not a gesture, not a word, not a breath,
Not a flicker of one line of your face.

You said: There is nothing I can do.
As you said it you seemed so proud.

*　　　*　　　*

There was a wretched danced with a wretched
The music began to burn.

*　　　*　　　*

In the chapel-cold porridge of fear
Crouched the spirit of Edward Lear
　　　Through the hole in his head
　　　His agony bled

Till he changed to a Whale
And spouted a hail –
Cholomondley Champagne and the best Babylonian
Beer.

*   *   *

To   Ian Hamilton and A. Alvarez, Poetry Reviewers –
Get your blue hands
off the hot skin of poetry.

*   *   *

My brain socialist
My heart anarchist
My eyes pacifist
My blood revolutionary

*   *   *

The man who believes in giraffes would swallow anything.
There's been nothing about ostriches in the papers for
   months, somebody's either building an ostrich monopoly
   or herding them into concentration camps.
Butterflies fly zigzag because they want to fly zigzag.
I have looked into a hedgehog's face and seen nothing but
   goodness.
A huge ram stamps his foot – a million sheep charge and
   occupy the Bradford Wool Exchange.

*   *   *

pip
pop
pip
pop
pip pip pip
pop

i am either a sound poet
or a bowl of Rice Crispies

*   *   *

(to a friend who killed himself)

All that pain
double-bulging under your forehead
I wish you could have taken
a handful of today's Yorkshire snow
and pressed it to that pain.
You rummaged for peace
in the green country, in the eye of the sun,
in visions of Tibet,
brain-shaking drugs, black magic,
police stations, among the stones,
beneath the stones.
But the stones, which seemed so calm,
screamed into life in your hurt hands.
Simpler than you
I simply wish you were alive
walking among this snowfall.
I'm glad that all your pain is dead.

*   *   *

(to dogmatic men and automatic dogs)

I'm an entrist, centrist, Pabloite workerist
– Sweet Fourth International and never been kissed,
I've got a mass red base that's why I'd rather sit on the floor,
If you want to be a vanguard, better join Securicor.

My daddy was opportunistic
My mama was mystified

I want to be a movement
But there's no one on my side . . .

*   *   *

Never look out
You might see something bigger than you
Never go out
You might get your iambics dirty

Wine is a river
Flowing down to sleep
So climb in the boat
With your legitimate wife
No sharks   No storms
No underwater explosions

Never look out
The sun might punch you in the eye –

Stay home.

*   *   *

I pulled on my solid granite gargoyle suit, borrowed a
   hunch from Sherlock Holmes and swung down from the
      turrets of Notre Dame just in time to rescue the
         naked Andromeda who was chained to King Kong
           in the middle of Red Square, Milwaukee.

Mark Antony immediately denounced me to a mob of
   Transylvanian peasants, who hurried me to the nearest
      oasis for a good guillotining.

Luckily for me the Flying Nun was power-diving down for
   a suicide raid on Moby Dick.

She noticed my plight, shot out a tentacle and scooped me
    into an echo chamber full of Dusty Springfields, thus
        foiling the machinations of Edgar Allen Fu Manchu,
            the Jackdaw of Zenda.

So you will understand why I am delighted to be here
    tonight to introduce a fourth member of fiction's
        Trolleybus Trinity – ladies and gentlemen, let's hear it
            for Miss Marlene Bronte.

*   *   *

At the end of each adventure
Mighty Mouse stands, arms folded, on a pedestal,
Cheered by a crowd of infant mice.

Every Sunday
God is praised
In several million churches.

Mighty Mouse saved us from the Monster Cat!!!!

*   *   *

In case the atmosphere catches on fire
The first thing to do will be to burn

*   *   *

Your breath is like deodorant, your blood like Irish lager,
Your idea of paradise an infinite *Forsyte Saga*,
Your head belongs to Nato and your heart to the Playboy
    Club,
You're the square root of minus zero, playing rub-a-dub-
    dub in a Fleet Street pub.

Sit tight in your tower of money . . .

You've got a problem of identity, ooh what an intellectual
    shame,
You've got a million pseudonyms and can't recall your
    maiden name,
You can't tell your face from your arse or your supper
    from your sex,
But you always remember who you are when it comes to
    signing cheques –

Sit tight in your tower of money . . .

*   *   *

In case England catches on fire
The first thing to do will be to form a committee
To organize a week-end seminar
On Little-Known Conflagrations in Italian History
Or The Rise and Fall of the Safety Match in Literature and
    Life.

*   *   *

Many thin men
saying: No.

But of course we've got to inside-out ourselves
and splash around in our own juice,
and the juice can't shine if you don't throw it up into the
    light,
and of course you're hard to hit if you keep dancing
and harder to hit if you make up your own dance as you
    dance,
and of course Tarzan is more exciting than Robert Larkin
because he can MOVE, swinging through jungles of
    clubfooted prose,
into your eye and out your navel,
and of course there's no perfect music,

– 169 –

no perfect words,
only the ridiculous beauty of man and woman
silly with each other,
pulling off their skins and swinging them round their heads,
becoming incredible fountains upon legs –

Many thin men
saying: No.

*   *   *

There's a factory for making factories,
A sinking pool for learning to drown,
A university like a pencil sharpener
To whittle you down to a pinpoint.
There's a mean old weather machine
Churning out crapstorms
And a generation gap between
Me and what I used to be.
But the cities of horror,
Skull pavements, murder girders –
They're going to crumble away in our hands.

*   *   *

The ice-cubes in my bloodstream decided to melt today.
I'd buy a moustache like everyone else
But I'm too attached to golden syrup.
There are hailstones as big as hailstones, but I'm sure
They're not aimed at me.
Yes, Timbuctoo. I suddenly want to go to Timbuctoo.

*   *   *

Grass pours down the hillside.
The stone wall gradually turns green.
A dead tree can keep its balance for years.

*   *   *

You can't win.
Mary Queen of Scots invented high heel shoes to make
    herself look taller they cut her bloody head off. (John
    Walton.)

                    *   *   *

Suddenly it hits me that it's May Day and I hadn't even
    noticed it was April,
And was gazing over the floodlit fields at a group of
    socially-minded cows,
And laughing to myself about the time Allen Ginsberg
    bared his arse to the people in a whizzing-by train,
And marking passages in a book of Fidel Castro's speeches –
Quote – And then you hear a revolutionary say: They
    crushed us,
They organized 200 radio programmes, so many
    newspapers,
so many magazines, so many TV shows,
so many of this and so many of that – and one wants to
    ask him,
What did you expect?
That they would put TV, radio, the magazines, the
    newspapers, the printing shops –
All this at your disposal?
Or are you unaware that these are the instruments of the
    ruling class
Designed explicitly for crushing the Revolution? –
unquote.
And I was also thinking of the pirhana fish grinning in the
    depths of my bank manager's soul,
And I was looking through the B.B.C. Folk Club
    magazine and trying to imagine the B.B.C. Folk,
And I was looking forward to a bit of bed with Celia in the
    afternoon,

And my eyes kept returning to a letter from the poet Tim
   Daly,
Liquid blue handwriting between strict blue lines,
His words saying – quote –
As a whole, the support I have received has amazed me,
I had anticipated only antagonism.
Love be praised, I was wrong – unquote –
And I look again at his address:
Her Majesty's Prison, County Road, Maidstone, Kent.
Tim, aged twenty-one, who took his petrol bombs
To the Imperial War Museum
Because the Museum was teaching children war . . .
And so when it suddenly hits me that it's been May Day
   all day
And I should be feeling solidarity,
I think yes so I should, and yes I do, and so yes I write this
   down
As a demonstration of solidarity –
With the cows, who have now moved on,
With Allen Ginsberg, who has now moved on,
With Fidel Castro as he moves socialism onwards,
With Celia who moves me as we move together,
And with Tim Daly the poet,
Locked away for four years
So that England may be safe for the dead.

Guns

They seem to have all the guns.
Most of the guns in Britain are
British/American government property
Police property
Or the property of gentry-gangsters
Who are British/American government property.

Nobody I love has a gun. Not in Britain.

The rich are rich because they fuck people about.
They call it the Quality of Leadership
And they have special school-machines producing
Leaders to fuck people about.

People with guns
Tend to fuck other people about.
The people they tend to fuck about
Are people who don't have guns.

None of my friends has a machine-gun ready,
Let alone a tank.

A few yards ahead of us, a row of truncheons.
Behind the truncheons, rifles,
Behind the rifles, grenades,
Behind the grenades, machine-guns,
Behind the machine-guns, tanks,
Behind the tanks, bombs,
And behind the bombs – the rich.

The rich are as stupid as guns.
They will be killed with their own guns.

In every capital
The fuckedabout of the world are taking arms.
The people of the world
Want the world.
We are going to take it.

PENGUINEWS AND
PENGUINS IN PRINT

Every month we issue an illustrated magazine, *Penguinews*. It's a lively guide to all the latest Penguins, Pelicans and Puffins, and always contains an article on a major Penguin author, plus other features of contemporary interest.

Penguinews is supplemented by *Penguins in Print*, a complete list of all the available Penguin titles – there are now over four thousand!

The cost is no more than the postage; so why not write for a free copy of this month's *Penguinews*? And if you'd like both publications sent for a year, just send us a cheque or a postal order for 30p (if you live in the United Kingdom) or 60p (if you live elsewhere), and we'll put you on our mailing list.

Dept EP, Penguin Books Ltd, Harmondsworth,
Middlesex.

Note: *Penguinews* and *Penguins in Print*
are not available in the U.S.A. or Canada

PENGUIN MODERN POETS

1* Lawrence Durrell Elizabeth Jennings R. S. Thomas

2* Kingsley Amis Dom Moraes Peter Porter

3* George Barker Martin Bell Charles Causley

4* David Holbrook Christopher Middleton David Wevill

5† Gregory Corso Lawrence Ferlinghetti Allen Ginsberg

6 George MacBeth Edward Lucie-Smith Jack Clemo

7* Richard Murphy Jon Silkin Nathaniel Tarn

8* Edwin Brock Geoffrey Hill Stevie Smith

9† Denise Levertov Kenneth Rexroth William Carlos Williams

10 Adrian Henri Roger McGough Brian Patten

11 D. M. Black Peter Redgrove D. M. Thomas

12* Alan Jackson Jeff Nuttall William Wantling

13 Charles Bukowski Philip Lamantia Harold Norse

14 Alan Brownjohn Michael Hamburger Charles Tomlinson

15 Alan Bold Edward Brathwaite Edwin Morgan

16 Jack Beeching Harry Guest Matthew Mead

17 W. S. Graham Kathleen Raine David Gascoyne

18 A. Alvarez Roy Fuller Anthony Thwaite

19 John Ashbery Lee Harwood Tom Raworth

20 John Heath-Stubbs F. T. Prince Stephen Spender

21* George Mackay Brown Norman MacCaig Iain Crichton Smith

*Not for sale in the U.S.A.

†Not for sale in the U.S.A. or Canada